TRUDEAU REVEALED

By His Actions and Words

David Somerville

Published by BMG Publishing Limited, 60A Industrial Road, Richmond Hill, Ontario, Canada, L4C 2Y1.

Printed in Canada by Webcom Limited, 3470 Pharmacy Avenue, Scarborough, Ontario. M1W 2P8.

BMG Publishing Limited
60A Industrial Road
Richmond Hill, Ontario
1978

Cover photograph courtesy of Toronto Sun.

ISBN 0-920254-04-7

Other titles from BMG
The National Dilemma and The Way Out
Red Maple—*How Canada Became the People's Republic of Canada in 1981*
Bilingual Today, French Tomorrow
Green Maple—*How Canada Could Attain Peace, Order and Good Government*

For My Father

Acknowledgments

I am grateful to the following publishers for permission to quote from the following books:

Macmillan of Canada's "André Laurendeau: Witness for Quebec" by André Laurendeau and "Quebec States Her Case" edited by Frank Scott and Michael Oliver:; James Lewis and Samuel's "The Asbestos Strike" edited by Pierre Elliott Trudeau; The Oxford University Press' "Approaches To Politics" by Pierre Elliott Trudeau and "Two Innocents in Red China" by Jacques Hébert and Pierre Elliott Trudeau; The University of Toronto Press' "Social Purpose For Canada" edited by Michael Oliver and "The Future of Canadian Federalism" edited by P.-A. Crépeau and C. B. McPherson.

I would like to thank the following libraries for their ready assistance: John P. Robarts Research Library; Central Reference Library of Metropolitan Toronto; Toronto Public Libraries; York University Law Library; Ontario Archives; Montreal Municipal Library; University of Montreal's Faculty of Social Science Library; National Library and National Archives, Ottawa; Ottawa Public Libraries; British Library, London; Centre Georges Pompidou Library, Paris and the libraries of the Toronto Sun, the Montreal Gazette and Le Monde, Paris.

I would also like to thank many individuals for their assistance, including those who granted me interviews.

Lastly, I thank my mother and father for their support and

encouragement, and Robert Charbonneau of Montreal and M. and Mme. Jacques Lafeuille of Paris for their help and hospitality, and Eric Lafeuille for his assistance in translating several particularly difficult passages from French into English.

Most of all, however, I would like to thank Jennifer O'Brian for her pluck and patience during my frequent absences and her cheerful support during a long year's labour.

Toronto, Ontario   David Somerville
March, 1978

Preface

On April 6 this year, Pierre Elliott Trudeau will have been Canada's prime minister for 10 years, at a time when this country and the world are in a state of turmoil.

Extraordinarily powerful states are turning nations into battle-fields. Beset with inflation, starvation and drought, terrorism, war and unemployment, nations, and their peoples, are being torn apart physically and spiritually by something which has no form or substance: ideology.

In a pitiless war that has continued for 60 years, the ideology which puts a premium on the individual and free enterprise has fought with another which stresses a monolithic state to serve the collective good.

That conflict has been exacerbated by resurgent nationalism in many countries, including Canada.

As his close friend Gerard Pelletier observed, Trudeau has spent his life formulating a coherent system of thought. He is, in fact, the most ideological prime minister this country has ever had.

But what are his ideologies? His belief in, and arguments for, the system of federalism were well known at the time he sought Lester Pearson's mantle in 1968. But that is only part of the picture.

It is painful and embarrassing, if not frightening, to re-read accounts of that leadership campaign of a decade ago. In it, the relationship between Trudeau and the public resembled more an adolescent infatuation than an electoral give-and-take.

Most reporters – if one may use the word that loosely – tried to outdo each other in mindless, and usually irrelevant, adulation. There was no need to. He had qualities which could have been praised in good conscience.

Reporters weren't content merely to say that Trudeau could do no wrong: anyone brave, or foolhardy enough to differ was subject to abuse of surprising violence.

The difficulty in examining a specific government policy in 1978, without referring to Trudeau's past and earlier ideas, is that it might be argued that the policy is a result of faceless civil servants or pressures beyond the government's control.

Only by knowing the past can we hope to understand the present and perhaps predict the future.

But what do Canadians know, really, about Trudeau's past? What did he study, believe, do and write in the 48 years before he became prime minister?

I was one of a group – which included Liberals – who had reservations about Trudeau in 1968. I could neither explain nor articulate them, but they were there.

Some asked, "Why doesn't anyone find out about his ideas, his past?"

By the fall of 1976 I decided to find out for myself. This book is the result. Except where otherwise indicated, translations from French are my own. I have tried to be objective, while admitting the difficulty of doing so.

If so many reporters had not betrayed their trust to inform readers, viewers and listeners as objectively as possible, years ago, this book would not have been written. It is an effort to straighten the record, to restore some balance.

I have not drawn conclusions, advocated courses of action or issued warnings.

After a year in power, this is what Prime Minister Trudeau said:

"I suppose one has to be in the wheelhouse to see what shifts are taking place. I know that we have spun the wheel and I know that the rudder is beginning to press against the waves and the sea ... but perhaps the observer, who is on the deck and smoking his pipe, or drinking his tea, sees the horizon much in the same direction and doesn't realize it, but perhaps he will find himself disembarking at a different island than the one he thought he was sailing for."

To Canadians, I say, this book is a chart: locate this "different island", and decide if it is the one upon which you wish to disembark.

David Somerville

Contents

CONTENTS

1

In the Beginning . . .

The smoke had cleared, the dead had been buried, the war was over, the battle done.

It was June, 1919: a 20-year ceasefire called the Treaty of Versailles was signed to end four years of deadlocked slaughter. The war to end all wars was over.

The terrible conflict had left its scars throughout western Europe in ravaged vineyards and pastures scored with trenches.

A less visible, but very real, scar had been left in the soul of Canada which had given up so many young men to the cause.

Two years earlier conscription had been made law and forced a crisis which virtually sundered the nation.

Latent racial antagonisms between French Canadians and English Canadians flared into a bitterness not witnessed since Britain had defeated France on the Plains of Abraham 160 years before.

It was into this unhappy world that Joseph Philippe Pierre Ives Elliott Trudeau was born on October 18.

Fate and history combined to bring the child into a world of contradictions, tensions and unreality.

His father, Jean-Charles Emile, was a bull-like, expansive, aggressive French Canadian whose forebear, Etienne Truteau, had arrived in Canada in 1659, exactly a century before the conquest.

Grace Elliott, his mother, was a gentle, retiring lady of culture and a product of United Empire Loyalist stock whose

1

family had originally fled to Canada after the American Revolution.

In those early post-war years in Canada, English Canadians were "those damned imperialist English" to many French Canadians, while to the former, French Canadians were those who had cut and run during the war when Canada needed them most.

Trudeau was neither one nor the other, and at the same time he was both.

In Quebec society of that era, the Roman Catholic church urged French Canadian men into one of three occupations: the church, law, or farming.

English Canadians were left to do the business and banking.

But Jean-Charles, or Charley as he was better known, didn't fit the mold. He went into business and succeeded in a big way mainly through raw drive and determination.

He succeeded to such an extent that by the time soup lines were forming at the beginning of the "Dirty Thirties" young Pierre was being chauffeured to school in the family Rolls.

But if wealth came quickly, it didn't come easily.

After Charley Trudeau had graduated from law school with fellow-classmate Maurice Lenoblet Duplessis, he began a practice with his friend and brother-in-law Charles-Edouard Guérin.

As business blossomed once more in a post-war boom so did the number of cars, unreliable and primitive though they were.

Charley, his partner and a few others started the Automobile Owners' Association in 1921. For ten dollars a year a subscriber was offered a road map, free and unlimited towing and discounts on gas and oil at designated service stations.

In 1922 Charley's second son was born, Charles Elliott. Added to Pierre, and a daughter Suzette, born in 1918, his wife and a house, Charley had his hands full.

To make matters worse, the AOA, at this point, hadn't really caught fire.

Had it not been for the generosity of Charley's father-in-law and several friends, it might have gone bankrupt. But he held on grimly and turned out more than once before dawn after a snow storm to drive a tow-truck and fasten tire chains.

2

It paid off. By 1925 the AOA had more than 10,000 members and a chain of gas and service stations throughout Montreal. Charley's partner wasn't as keen on the business as he was so they worked an even trade – Guérin got Trudeau's share of the law practice and Trudeau took Guérin's share of the AOA.

As the twenties roared on, so did Charley and his business.

Newly-found spare time was devoted to newly-found friends in the business community during hunting and fishing trips to the Club Chapleau in the Laurentians, hockey and baseball games and boxing matches.

But he still found time for his family.

By this time young Pierre was going to the English section of Querbes primary school where he sometimes got into fisticuffs with young French Canadian boys, Michel Chartrand among them.

When he arrived home after school he usually found his father there to help him with homework. He remembered his father as a man "rather formidable . . . rather authoritarian . . . very intelligent . . . very quick . . . very strong."

After a little homework and conversation with his children, Charley would retire to the Club St. Denis, which he had joined in 1927. There he sat down with some high-rollers from the growing French Canadian business community to play poker into the wee hours of the morning for stakes running into the thousands of dollars.

During the summer the whole family vacationed at a summer house near Mont Tremblant in the Laurentians, north of Montreal.

In 1928, the family started going to Old Orchard on the coast of Maine for two months each summer, Charley would visit on weekends to take his children swimming, hiking and canoeing and generally indulging his passion for sports.

Then disaster struck again.

Ten years after the treaty had been signed, and five days after Pierre's tenth birthday, it happened: Black Friday, 1929.

The market crashed and frenzied selling began. Charley's friends suddenly found that their paper wealth wasn't worth the paper it was printed on.

Charley was more fortunate. There were still cars on the road, and they were still breaking down.

He bought shares in Hollinger Mines, Algoma Steel, a third of Belmont Park, Montreal's Coney Island, some of De Lorimier Stadium and, for $15,000, one fifth of the Montreal Royals baseball franchise.

While the western world was gripped in the throes of the depression, Charley was riding high. He had a comfortable brownstone house in Outremont, an exclusive French Canadian enclave in Montreal, with maid and chauffeur, a good wife and three healthy, intelligent children.

In 1931 he sold the AOA to Standard Oil's Canadian subsidiary, Imperial Oil, for more than one million dollars, and was retained as manager of the business.

The sale did not go through without a hitch, however.

Charley was charged with a tax irregularity arising from the sale and was convicted. He appealed the ruling all the way to the Supreme Court of Canada before the judgement was overturned.

Despite the crash and the depression, Charley had obviously found that the system of free enterprise and capitalism worked, at least for him. But there was a group of young Canadian left-wing intellectuals who disagreed and a year after Charley had made his killing in the sale of the AOA they formed a third national political party in Canada, the socialist Co-operative Commonwealth Federation.

About the same time, in Germany, a demagogic ex-corporal named Adolf Hitler was also preparing a political move.

While he ranted and bluffed and schemed, a despot named Stalin was killing millions of Russian peasants while bending them to his system. And all the while western democracies were busy dismantling their armies.

Storm clouds had begun gathering again.

In Montreal, though, it was sunny.

Young Pierre was sent to the elite Jesuit classical college, Jean de Brébeuf for his secondary education in French.

The college was named after an early Jesuit missionary to Canada who was tortured and burnt at the stake. With icy self-

4

control Jean de Brébeuf uttered not a word throughout his ordeal.

At the age of 12, young Pierre was immersed in the Jesuit atmosphere devoted to excellence and self-control, physical, intellectual and emotional.

One school-mate, Pierre Vadboncoeur, recalls that the Jesuit demand for self-discipline and control "fitted him like a glove".

Another development in his character began when Pierre Trudeau, during his early adolescence, started to withdraw into himself. He demanded, somehow needed, a private world untouched by others.

In the summer of '33 Charley took the whole family on a grand tour of Europe and young Pierre saw the Nazis and Fascists at first hand, but it didn't leave much of an impression.

"All I noticed were the fanfares and the soldiers and the motorcycles and all that. At the age of fourteen, I obviously didn't see the political significance of it all," he later recalled.

Upon their return, Charley plunged once more into business, including his baseball franchise, of which he was the vice-president. The team wasn't doing very well and in early 1935 Charley and his wife travelled to Orlando, Florida to watch the team going through its paces during spring training.

When Grace returned to Montreal, Charley stayed behind, having decided to travel with the team for part of the season. In early April he was out in a spring rain and caught a cold which turned into pneumonia.

Grace and Suzette flew down on April 10 and reached his side only hours before his death.

One obituary summed up the man the best: "He was full of spit and damn good fun."

Life went on for Pierre. He excelled at Brébeuf in studies and sports. He was always at, or near, the top of his class and won a name as a daring and competent skier.

Except for lacrosse, which he played as roughly as anyone, Trudeau stayed away from team sports.

Francois Hertel, a teacher at the college, remembers he would accompany Grace to hockey games for which she had season's tickets, instead of Pierre.

"My son is too intellectual to enjoy them," she would say.

Hertel had a special relationship with young Trudeau. Jesuit teachers at the college were celibate and most were obsessed with sex, said Hertel, which Trudeau didn't find attractive.

One day after class young Trudeau came to him for guidance.

"Why did you come to me?" asked Hertel.

"I know that you never talk about tail," the 18-year-old Trudeau replied.

Hertel wasn't only interested in teaching, but in "giving a sense – a direction – to the students' life."

He was known as a "free-thinker" and gave informal lectures after school hours on philosophers "not officially approved" to students, among them Trudeau.

Most Jesuit teachers were nationalists, he said, and so was Trudeau, although not fanatically so. "He was more for the French Canadian than against the English Canadian," said Hertel.

He sometimes came to the Trudeau house on McCulloch Street for Sunday evening soirées which were accompanied by recorded or live classical music.

It was during these years that Trudeau made a name for himself as a fighter. His father had taken his son to private boxing lessons, and apparently Pierre learned them well. There are several stories of fist fights during these years, but none have him losing.

It was perhaps just as well that young Pierre had learned to box. Flashes of Trudeau come through as being arrogant and insufferable in his relations with other students.

Jean de Grandpré was a classmate. He became president of his year at Brébeuf with Trudeau as vice-president.

"Outstanding as his accomplishments were, there were other students in the class who equalled him and challenged his abilities," he said.

"In such a group Trudeau did not appear as extraordinary as he might have elsewhere."

He said that although Trudeau was "well-liked" at the college, he "kept his distance" and displayed a "certain arrogance which even then led him to ridicule people who were not too bright".

De Grandpré also described him as a "dilettante . . . spoiled brat . . . intellectual snob and lone wolf".

In his last year or two at Brébeuf, Trudeau met Gerard Pelletier and his girl friend – and later wife – Alexandrine Leduc.

Pelletier remembers they were all shocked when the Roman Catholic church in Quebec supported the Franco faction, backed by Hitler and Mussolini, in the Spanish Civil War.

Pelletier said Alexandrine had read a French review called Esprit which opposed Franco, and introduced Esprit to him and Trudeau. The review, its founder and editors were to figure largely in the later lives of both Pelletier and Trudeau.

About the same time that Franco and part of the army revolted against the government, Charley Trudeau's old classmate, Maurice Duplessis came to power in Quebec as head of the National Union party. That was August 1937.

An avowed anti-communist, within a year he had passed the Padlock Law, which allowed police to seize communist propaganda and padlock the premises where it was found.

By Trudeau's second last year in Brébeuf, 1938, events were moving swiftly in the world. Hitler, now in complete control of Germany, demanded lebensraum – living space. He annexed Austria and threatened Czechoslovakia's Sudetenland.

Mussolini grabbed Albania and the western democracies finally started waking up.

British Prime Minister Neville Chamberlain helped sell out the Sudetenland at a Munich conference in September, 1938, for "peace in our time".

He gained less than a year of it.

In August, 1939, Stalin and Hitler shocked the world by concluding a ten-year non-aggression pact, and, on the first day of September, Hitler's tanks dashed through Poland in a lightning strike.

By the time Trudeau celebrated his 20th birthday, Poland had been overrun.

Canada was once more at war.

2

War

With determination and drive, Canada mobilized for the war, more united than most had dared hope.

Less than a week after its declaration of war, the Canadian nation seemed to have worked a compromise between English and French Canadians which would avert the terrible division over conscription.

The Liberal government of Prime Minister MacKenzie King promised the French Canadians there would be no conscription for overseas service, and they, in turn, promised to support the war effort.

Shortly before the disaster at Dunkirk, King reaffirmed his promise, called an election for a war mandate and was swept to power in March, 1940.

If the great body of Canadians were united, there was a small but vociferous opposition composed of widely disparate groups.

Adrien Arcand's fascist group in Quebec was interned along with the Communist Party of Canada, both of whom, for different reasons, virulently opposed the Canadian war effort.

Pierre Trudeau was completing his last year at Brébeuf and shared the same attitude as many other French Canadians of his age. The war was distant and didn't really concern him, but he would put up with it.

Almost imperceptibly, feelings in English Canada began to harden. As tens of thousands of young men east and west of Quebec joined the forces and were shipped overseas, some began to wonder if French Canada was really pulling its weight.

Then, once again, Canada went through the same gut-churning, torturous experience as in the previous war.

On January 22, 1942, the King government announced it would hold a plebiscite asking the Canadian people to release it from its anti-conscription pledge.

Conservative English Canadians, who wanted immediate conscription without a plebiscite, cried "Treason!"

French Canadians, who recalled King's earlier promise, shouted "Criminal!"

King emphasized that it wasn't a question of bringing in conscription, necessarily.

"Conscription if necessary, but not necessarily conscription," was how he put it.

The date for the plebiscite was set at April 27 and the wording for it was cagey, if not misleading. It read:

"Are you in favour of releasing the government from any obligation arising out of any past commitments restricting the methods of raising men for military service?"

Passions continued to flare, aided by men such as Colin Gibson, King's minister of national revenue, who said, "As I see it – Hitler would vote 'No,' [to the plebiscite] Quisling would not vote, and Canadians will vote 'Yes.'"

For his part, Trudeau was not swept up in the first surges of bitterness. He enlisted in the Canadian Officers' Training Corps as required in his final year of Brébeuf.

As long as he kept his marks up, Trudeau would not be inducted into a regular military unit in Canada. So, twice a week he paraded at Jean de Brébeuf college for lectures and drill.

In the fall of 1940 he enrolled in the faculty of law at the University of Montreal, but was kept with the Brébeuf detachment of the COTC.

Trudeau was a less than ideal recruit.

Jacques Prince instructed Trudeau and a group of young Brébeuf recruits on military law, leadership and the like. The general attitude, as he recalled, was somewhat cavalier.

"We took it as sport – we had to do it and we tried to have the most fun we could."

Trudeau frequently gave him trouble.

9

"I threw him out three or four times for disobeying orders. I would tell the group to turn right and he would turn left." But Trudeau wasn't the only one to give him trouble.

Prince said Trudeau usually "looked like he never took things seriously – but don't believe it. He took in everything, he remembered everything, heard everything."

Jean Lamontagne, the commanding officer of the COTC for all Jesuit colleges, remembered Trudeau in the same way.

"His face is the same today as it was then – you thought he was laughing at you, but he wasn't.

"He was the brightest we ever had and he never worried about promotion."

At that time, extended specialist training for army officers was being given in English only at centres outside Quebec.

Lamontagne wanted to find out which COTC candidates were bilingual enough to continue on the specialized courses if the need arose.

He personally conducted an unofficial, verbal survey of all the recruits and found Trudeau, at age 21, was by the far the most bilingual recruit.

The recruits were generally a good bunch, he said. "We chose to ignore the pranks. We figured if they were pulling pranks they would be good soldiers. We didn't kick out anybody – we were proud of that."

During the summers Trudeau and the group went for training at Camp Farnham, about 45 miles south-east of Montreal.

When he wasn't drilling, doing field tactics or marching 15 miles to St. Bruno for target practice, Trudeau was up to his old tricks.

He and several others formed a group that put on comedy performances in the evening. One night Trudeau turned up in the group's hut with "The Commandos" written across the front of his cap and the rest of his group followed suit.

A friend recalled that a senior officer walked in, saw their caps and shouted "What the hell have you got on your caps?

"You're not commandos – get it off by tomorrow morning."

The next morning all of the group except one had taken it off

– Trudeau. He had added a word to his cap so that it read, "Not the Commandos".

That was the final straw. He and his fellow "commandos" were put on what was called "Drill for Recalcitrants" or DR.

Jacques Prince, their old instructor from Brébeuf was detailed to put them to work, and he took them to an ammunition truck which needed loading.

A beefy English Canadian NCO bellowed something to the effect of "Get your idle bodies moving there and get those boxes loaded!" Everyone in the group hopped to it – except one.

Trudeau stood to one side, doing nothing. The NCO came up to him and started berating him.

"Je ne parle pas anglais," said the perfectly bilingual Trudeau.

Smiling, Prince interpreted for the NCO and Trudeau looked at Prince, surprised, and replied in perfect English, "If he had only used a clearer expression I would have understood."

The taunting didn't stop there. Trudeau turned up for morning inspections with his battledress blouse hitched up on his arms and waist.

An inspecting officer would come up to him and ask him if his blouse was too small.

"Yes, I think it is," Trudeau would reply, and an NCO would dutifully note the fact that Trudeau needed a larger blouse.

Then, just as the inspecting officer began to move away, Trudeau would let the blouse fall naturally to his wrists and waist and exclaim, "No, it seems to fit!"

Sometimes the whole group got into the act. They were told that when they heard a bell sounding they were to report immediately to the centre of camp.

By chance, the next time the bell sounded, the "commandos" were all in the shower, and dutifully reported to the centre of camp – stark naked.

Rivalries between the French and English Canadians on "civvy street" were brought to camp as well. Even Prince, as an instructor, was swept up in it.

"One night about 10 p.m. there were about ten guys from the McGill COTC in a big wooden W.C. outside," Prince recalled.

He, Trudeau and at least 15 others gathered around it and "Oomph! We turned it over!" said Prince. "They came out in a hurry."

All in all, as one of the "commandos" put it, "we were really bad soldiers".

But there were other French Canadians who voluntarily became superb soldiers and laid down their lives.

When Russia was invaded by the Nazis in June, 1941 and found herself hard-pressed she demanded the allies open a second front in Europe to relieve the pressure. The Nazi invasion produced an ironic sidelight in Canada.

Communists who had been interned were released and overnight became heated, energetic supporters of the war effort. Fred Rose, a communist member of parliament, appeared on hustings with a French Canadian, Jean-Louis Gagnon, to call for even greater efforts to crush the Nazis—late partners in a non-aggression pact.

The allies' answer to Russia's demand was a doomed raid on the French town of Dieppe by a mainly Canadian force August 19, 1942.

Part of the raiding force was the Montreal regiment, Les Fusiliers de Montréal, which Trudeau was eventually to join.

Ironically, one of the minor objectives which the force succeeded in temporarily liberating was Varengeville, the family seat of Trudeau's uncle, Gordon Elliott.

Trudeau didn't stay out of the storm of controversy swirling around the decision to hold a plebiscite on the issue of overseas conscription.

When the League for the Defence of Canada was formed in early 1942 to campaign for a rejection of conscription he became deeply involved.

The leaders of the League were men Trudeau would know and work with many years later. André Laurendeau was the League's principal executive officer, and the editor of the nationalist review, National Action.

Gerard Filion was another influential member and represented the Catholic Union of Farmers. Jean Drapeau and Roger Varin represented youth movements in the League.

Memberships in the movement were sold for a dollar each and Laurendeau claimed tens of thousands of members.

The most influential French Canadian newspaper, Le Devoir, gave the League strong support and as contributions rolled in a radio campaign was organized.

Maurice Duplessis' National Union gave the movement passive support and local committees sprang up in smaller centres throughout Quebec.

The League set February 11, 1942, as the date for its first public meeting and it was to prove a fiery baptism for the fledgling movement.

A crowd of 10,000 supporters filled the St. Jacques Market in Montreal and spilled onto the street outside. The League's president, Dr. J. B. Prince, took the platform with Gerard Filion, Jean Drapeau and Maxime Raymond, a federal Liberal M.P.

Trudeau was one of the hundreds of students standing outside the market trying to hear the speeches over loudspeakers rigged for the occasion. But the loudspeakers weren't working properly and the situation deteriorated when empty streetcars continued to roll noisily past the crowd.

Soon pieces of ice and bricks began to fly and the trams' windows were broken. Police gathered while a group of nearby soldiers were heard to say "This is an English country. These Frenchmen should be speaking English."

When students swept into a nearby brothel and turfed out startled patrons the police charged on motorcycles. The students appeared to calm down a little, but then broke into chants of "Down With the Gazette", an English newspaper in Montreal.

Detectives were dispatched to protect the buildings of English newspapers while the whole police force turned out on foot, horse and motorcycle to contain the students.

A friend who was with Trudeau during the riot, Gaetan Robert, recalled "We were so much against conscription that we would try to break up rallies in support of the Allies. Trudeau and I and some other friends would come prepared, with bits of metal inside our hats in case the police hit us."

"Once we tried to smash the windows at the Gazette building," he said.[1]

The plebiscite produced the result everyone had been expecting. Quebec voted overwhelmingly against conscription while Canada outside Quebec voted even more solidly for conscription.

Canada was once more divided.

The League's activities didn't stop after the plebiscite, and neither did Trudeau's. He was an editor of the University of Montreal student newspaper, Quartier Latin, when he wrote a cutting article against conscription in November, 1942.

He headlined the article "Nothing Matters Except Victory," a quote from King. A note at the top told the reader that the censors passed it only because its exaggeration rendered it "perfectly inoffensive".

Tongue firmly in cheek, from his imaginary ivory tower, Trudeau lectured the students, ". . we're not happy with you. More than once, you have profoundly saddened us . . .

"But last year you went too far . . . Just a short while ago you mocked and scorned our great politicians, in defiance of their wisdom so agreeable to our powerful Allies.

"You were rebels during the plebiscite. Young men, this can't go on. I will even add that it has got to stop.

"We could shut down the subversive publication 'Quartier Latin' . . . it would be easy for us to ban all student gatherings and deprive you of the Canadian Officers' Training Corps which you find so idiotic . . . and you would soon be called up.

"But happily we know, deep down, that you are sensible, reasonable people.

"We know it's impossible, but let's just suppose that England had dealt wrongly with us French Canadians . . . when the enemy, without provocation, carries the war into our waters, is this the time to recall childish divisions? How can you dream about minority rights? Talk about economic favoritism? Agitate on questions of decentralization, education and religion?

"Dear friends, my dear, good little friends . . . if all this nonsense had any importance we'd be the first ones to busy ourselves with it."

After exhorting the students against the "MONSTER OF BERLIN" and the "NAZI HORDES" Trudeau concluded with, "But don't thank me for this lesson in public-spiritedness.

14

"To have done my duty is thanks enough. I would give my life if that would aid the sublime cause of the United Nations [the Allies] – yes! I would give my life to writing."[2]

Only five days after his article, Trudeau made his own contribution to an effort to defeat a cabinet minister in Prime Minister King's government, General L. R. Laflèche. He was standing for by-election in the riding of Outremont.

The League had put up Jean Drapeau as a candidate against him with Michel Chartrand as his campaign manager. On the evening of November 25 the League held an election rally in the Lajoie school hall where Chartrand, Drapeau, D'Iberville Fortier and Trudeau spoke.

It was a wildly enthusiastic crowd, overflowing the hall, which heard Trudeau rail against the general.

They didn't necessarily have to vote for Drapeau, Trudeau told the crowd, but they had to vote against Laflèche.

"The general is campaigning in his uniform," he said. "In a democracy, I was taught, you present yourself as a citizen, and not as the representative of a military clique . . . using reflected glory."

He accused the government of resorting to "tricks" and disgusting dishonesty" and asked rhetorically, "You say that the King cabinet knows what measures to take?

"In a democracy, the people are hardly ever mistaken. And if we aren't in a democracy, then let's start the revolution without delay.

"The government is made up of traitors and honest men. The latter are divided between those who want conscription for the same reason they want the war and those who want it simply out of stupidity."

The government's policies were "idiotic" when they weren't "disgusting," said Trudeau.

"The government declared war at a time when North America wasn't menaced with invasion, at a time when Hitler hadn't yet won his lightning victories.

"The people are being asked to commit suicide. Citizens of Quebec, don't be content to complain. Long live freedom's flag! Enough of patchwork solutions, now is the time for cataclysms!"[3]

15

Chartrand, his wife and Trudeau went one other evening to a campaign meeting of the opposition at the parish hall of St. Jean de la Croix, which had a number of senators and members of parliament present.

Chartrand recalled that his wife was very pregnant at the time, but she nevertheless began heckling one of the speakers.

"A big bouncer came up and told her to keep quiet," Chartrand recalled. "Trudeau played the knight.

"He wanted to take the defence of a pregnant woman but he got kicked out by the bouncers."

Despite all their efforts, Laflèche won the election with almost double the vote of Drapeau. Trudeau went back to his studies.

He disciplined himself and worked as hard at law as he had at Brébeuf. One fellow student and friend recalled that his timetable was tight.

"He would call me and say, "It is now 7.10 p.m. I would like to walk with you until a quarter to eight. Is that possible?' "

Trudeau bought a big Harley-Davidson motorcycle and raced around Montreal and the Quebec countryside with another rich young man, Roger Rolland, who also had a Harley.

One afternoon in Trudeau's final year of law, they were at Rolland's house and he dragged out two World War One uniforms, one French, the other German, complete with helmets.

Rolland donned the German uniform and Trudeau the French one. Then they raced off to the country to surprise some friends staying at St. Adolphe de Howard.[4]

Along the way they stopped at a large house in Ste. Agathe. When a maid answered the door Trudeau demanded "Wasser". When he insisted Rolland try the water first to see if it was poisoned, he tasted it and fell to the ground, gasping and writhing. The maid fled and the two mounted and drove off, with Rolland in the lead.

Trudeau hadn't gone far when an old man flagged him down and, obviously thinking Rolland was a real German, pointed after him and said "He went that way!"

That wasn't the only way Trudeau let off steam, however. He had become involved in canoeing in a big way. In the summer

16

of 1941 he paddled 1,000 miles to Hudson Bay with a friend, Guy Viau.

Trudeau had insisted that Viau have his appendix removed before the trip, saying it was stupid to risk an attack of appendicitis hundreds of miles from civilization.

Viau dutifully had an appendectomy. It was only later that he learned that Trudeau had never had his removed.

Trudeau wrote an article in Jeunesse Étudiante Catholique, a magazine edited by his friend, Gerard Pelletier, in which he described his passion for canoeing. It provides a rare, fleeting glimpse of his soul.

"What sets a canoeing expedition apart is that it purifies you more rapidly and inescapably than any other. Travel a thousand miles by train and you are a brute; pedal five hundred on a bicycle and you remain basically a bourgeois; paddle a hundred in a canoe and you are already a child of nature.

"You entrust yourself, stripped of your worldly goods, to nature. Canoe and paddle, blanket and knife, salt pork and flour, fishing rod and rifle; that is about the extent of your wealth. To remove all the useless material baggage from a man's heritage is, at the same time, to free his mind from petty preoccupations, calculations and memories.

"You learn that your best friend is not your rifle, but someone who shares a night's sleep with you after ten hours of paddling at the other end of a canoe . . .

"You return not so much a man who reasons more, but a more reasonable man. For, throughout this time, your mind has learned to exercise itself in the working conditions which nature intended. Its primordial role has been to sustain the body in the struggle against a powerful universe."[5]

Perhaps it was the same force which sent him on marathon canoe trips that made him give up law after articling for less than a year at Hyde and Ahern, a well-known Montreal firm.

In any case, after being called to the bar he decided to pursue his studies in political economy and government at Harvard University, in Cambridge, Massachusetts.

Trudeau found the courses at Harvard under such men as Karl Friedrich and W. Y. Elliott both demanding and specialized.

Another Canadian student, Fred Gibson remembered him as a "very articulate, independent-minded, critical, amusing, detached but very interested person".

Trudeau was critical about the quality of his previous university education. "The majors in political science there had read more about Roman Law and Montesquieu than I had as a lawyer," he later said.

While at Harvard, Trudeau seems to have gone through a crisis of conscience.

He wrote a letter to his friend of Jean de Brébeuf years in Montreal, Pierre Vadboncoeur, asking him for advice.

According to Vadboncoeur Trudeau was considering giving away his personal fortune. Vadboncoeur says he wrote back and "told him not to give away the money because he would probably get into politics and he'd need his financial independence".

Trudeau settled into a dormitory in Hastings Hall and was soon joined by René Cousineau, another French Canadian from Montreal, who was studying economics.

"He wore a beret at Harvard," Cousineau recalled. "He wanted it known he was French. People called him names but that didn't bother him. He liked to provoke opinions.

"He was very well disciplined, he had a work program and went to the gym two or three times each week but still found time for everything.

"I teased him because he wanted to make a political career – he used to tell me he would never make a compromise on his ideas. He was interested in politics from the social point of view, he was a reformer."

Trudeau was taking a course under Professor Joseph Schumpeter on economic theory and banking, and must have read Schumpeter's book first published only two years earlier, "Capitalism, Socialism and Democracy".[6]

In it, Schumpeter wrote, "I have tried to show that a socialist form of society will inevitably emerge from an equally inevitable decomposition of capitalist society."

He also noted that "the transition from the capitalist to the socialist order will always raise problems . . ."[7]

Schumpeter then described how the transition could be made in societies of different stages of development.

In Trudeau's second year, an associate from the University of Montreal's law faculty, Pierre Carrignan, arrived in Harvard and looked him up.

"I went to his room in a student dormitory there. On the door was written 'Pierre Elliott Trudeau – Citizen of the World.'

"When he was in his room he didn't answer anybody, he worked so hard. To get in we had to slip a piece of paper below the door saying, 'we want to see you!' "

The two years of study were soon and successfully completed, and after a summer's break, he sailed across the Atlantic to begin further studies at the Sorbonne in France.

FOOTNOTES CHAPTER 2

1. Ann Charney, "Pierre Elliott Trudeau: The Myth and The Reality," in "Their Turn to Curtsy—Your Turn to Bow," edited by Peter Newman and Stan Fillmore, MacLean-Hunter Ltd., 1972.
2. Quartier Latin, November 20, 1942.
3. Le Devoir, November 26, 1942.
4. Although other published accounts differ, Rolland insists it was he who wore the German uniform, not Trudeau.
5. This article originally appeared in the November, 1944 edition of JEC, but was quoted in translation from "Wilderness Canada," edited by Borden Spears, Clarke, Irwin and Co. Ltd., 1970.
6. Joseph Schumpeter, "Capitalism, Socialism and Democracy," Harper and Row, New York, 1975, p. xiii.
7. Ibid., p. 219.

3

The Formative Years

Trudeau arrived in the "City of Light" a little more than a year after its liberation from five years of darkness under the Nazis.

Paris is a great, enchanting city, a home for writers and artists as well as its vibrant, noisy throngs.

In the autumn the crisp air and the smoky scent of chestnuts roasting in streetcorner braziers produce a mellow, hazy magic which the 28-year-old Trudeau must have felt.

Times were still a little thin for the city's populace. Bakeries were almost back in full production and bread rationing was just being ended. Fuel and some other commodities were still being carefully conserved.

The war had left a residue of bitterness between many Frenchmen who had aided the resistance and risked their lives, and others who had collaborated with the Nazis under Marshal Pétain.

Charles de Gaulle, the wartime leader of the Free French Forces who had led a column into Paris in 1944, came to power with the help of the communists, who had been active in the underground.

In return for their electoral support, de Gaulle had promised them cabinet posts.

Trudeau arrived with a group of other French Canadian students including Roger Rolland, Guy Viau, Marcel Rioux, Andrée

Desautels, Jean-Marc Léger, Edmond Labelle, Marcel Blais and Jean-Louis Roux. All were partially supported in their studies by a grant from the Quebec government.

Rioux recalled he and Viau shared room 40 in the Maison du Canada while Trudeau and Rolland had room 39.

The group soon settled into a local café, "Le Pommier Norman", where they became such regulars that they kept their serviettes in napkin rings and were able to put away a half-finished bottle of wine for their next meal.

Rioux remembers being embarrassed on occasions when Trudeau, who with Rolland had brought his Harley-Davidson to Paris and was obviously well-off, would carefully scrutinize his bill after a meal.

But at other times Trudeau would say to him, "Do you think so-and-so could use a few dollars?" Sure enough, not long afterward, said Rioux, "so-and-so" would anonymously receive some money to keep him going.

They were a lively group. Rioux recalled one night when Blais had left the Maison for a short trip to London.

Rolland and Trudeau grabbed a bronze bust of a former Canadian ambassador to France and laid it in Blais' bed, its greenish hue stark and horrible on the white pillow.

Friends were told Blais had met with a terrible accident on his way to London and asked to stay with the body in the room until dawn when the undertaker would arrive.

They arrived in the room and prayed for hours by candlelight. It was only when Blais stalked into the room, having returned prematurely from his trip, that the joke was discovered.

The group went on walking tours and trips to Normandy, where Trudeau visited his uncle Gordon Elliott, in Varengeville, which had been briefly liberated during the Canadian raid on Dieppe.

Elliott had fled his home during the war and served at the Royal Canadian Air Force base at Cap de la Madeleine near Three Rivers, Quebec, only returning home to his landscaping business when France was liberated.

Just before Christmas, after the group had decided to go on a ski trip to Mégève, Trudeau, Rolland and some others were sitting in Le Pommier Norman.

It was there that Trudeau, five years after persuading Viau to have his appendix out for their canoe trip, had an attack of appendicitis. He was rushed to the American Hospital for an appendectomy.

That didn't keep him from the Mégève trip, however. He hobbled onto the train and according to Rolland went skiing at least once.

Early in the new year another outing by Rolland and Trudeau almost landed Trudeau in jail.

University students staged their own Mardi Gras February 18, the day before Ash Wednesday, to let off steam. The parade started off peacefully enough about 11 a.m. down the Rue de L'Opéra, Rolland remembers, but the students soon started getting rowdy.

Rolland's own contribution was flicking the taxis' meter flags, which were mounted on the outside of the cabs, back to zero, much to the consternation of the drivers.

But as he was passing the Sorbonne he did it once too often and an enraged taxi driver leapt out in hot pursuit of a rapidly disappearing Rolland. He ran into the university and soon lost his pursuer in the labyrinthine halls.

Other students were well-stocked with bottles of talcum powder and sprayed the drivers of passing cars. Rolland said one student went up to a stopped limousine, opened the front door and doused an immaculate chauffeur while a lone passenger in the back seat looked on in disbelief.

By the time the parade reached the Champs Elysées in mid-afternoon it had swollen to 3,000 students and caused a massive traffic jam. The police decided it had gone on long enough. They moved in with truncheons and capes lined with lead weights for added punch.

Rolland prudently decided it was time to call it a day when the police chief of the arrondissement told them to disperse, and he left by a side street. He looked back to see Trudeau standing motionless in the middle of the boulevard.

Trudeau later told him he was arrested and bundled into the back of a paddy wagon with about a dozen other stubborn students. When they arrived at the police station, Trudeau waited until the last and then got out to see a sizable crowd and quite a commotion.

He sauntered forward and clapped the shoulder of a student in front of him and shook his hand.

"It's really been most enjoyable but I'm afraid I really can't stay," Trudeau told the student, glancing at his watch.

"You see, I have a dinner engagement. Goodbye."

With that he walked into the crowd and started running for the nearest subway station. The police soon noticed they were one student short and set out in pursuit, but luckily for Trudeau, there was a train just arriving and he dove in.

The doors closed just as the police arrived on the platform. As the train pulled out, Trudeau raised his hand and calmly thumbed his nose at them.

Trudeau had a lot of time for diversions as he didn't spend much time in his law classes or at the School of Political Science.

"Political science wasn't very far advanced in Paris at that time nor was political economy," he later said.

"I had just left Harvard and, in all modesty, knew more about these subjects than most of my professors. So, classes didn't interest me very much."

Rolland said bluntly, "I would qualify that year as a sabbatical year for him".

If Trudeau didn't find the professors very competent, he didn't find the students very attractive.

"In the School of Political Science a lot of the students, if not the majority, were reactionary sons of the great and petty bourgeois class, only worried about the prestige that a university diploma would get them."[2]

For Trudeau there was much more to university life than a diploma and its prestige.

Trudeau by this time was showing an intense interest in politics. Once he organized a discussion group in his room on the division of federal and provincial powers in Canada. Rolland recalled that "he was already a fund of knowledge on Canada at that time. He could reel off the history of the railways in Canada or quote from any given speech by Sir John A. Macdonald."

Jean-Paul Geoffroy, who had first met Trudeau when they were both confined to barracks during their COTC training, was studying nears Lyons at the time.

He recalls visiting Paris regularly and meeting with Trudeau, Jean-Luc Pépin and Pierre Juneau.

"Trudeau's thinking at that time was directed toward autonomy for Quebec," said Geoffroy. "We used to hold meetings to discuss it . . . he had an open mind."

Another regular visitor to Paris was Gerard Pelletier, who worked as secretary to the International Student Service on the Rue Calvin in Geneva. He described his job as "giving money to countries about to go communist".

He met students in the course of his work from France, Italy, Austria and Czechoslovakia and found them generally optimistic "except for the bourgeois youth who are gloomily watching their last privileges disappear".

On the other hand, Pelletier found that "the working class youth is very lively, drawing its energy from some left-wing parties which have allowed the worker to come of age".

Later in Canada, continuing student work, he would meet Mason Wade, Jean Beetz, Paul Fox, André Laurendeau and Maurice Sauvé.

It was during that year in Paris that Trudeau, and Pelletier during his visits, met Emmanuel Mounier, the founder of Esprit, whose work they had read at the urging of Alexandrine Leduc in 1938.

Mounier had founded the Catholic review only six years earlier, but it had grown quickly until it was published in three languages. By that time it figured largely in a crusade against the Franco faction in the Spanish Civil War.

Mounier and his review did so in the face of official church opposition, which was either silent on the issue or pro-Franco mainly because the loyalists were armed and supported by the communists.

Esprit became one of the main focal points for a movement in France called the Catholics of the Left, which was often in the centre of a storm of controversy over church-state relations.

Pelletier recalled that he and Trudeau "were really close to what they called the Catholics of the Left in France. It was because of Emmanuel Mounier who was a really great guy."

Mounier's cohorts at Esprit were Henri-Irenée Marrou, a regular contributor, Albert Béguin, the publisher and Jean-Marie Domenach, the editor-in-chief.

Jean-Marc Léger recalls meeting Domenach at Esprit, with Jean-Luc Pépin and D'Iberville Fortier.

"Esprit had a very great influence on all of us," he said. "It may not have been the greatest, but it was certainly the first."

Rolland remembers Trudeau meeting Mounier "a couple of times" and says "Trudeau and Pelletier were very much impressed by Esprit".

"Marrou was very much a Catholic of the Left," said Rioux. "He always wrote for Esprit. We knew him well in those days."

Members of the group in Paris saw different facets of the "Catholics of the Left" movement and Mounier's philosophy.

"You must accept certain aspects of communism and Marxist criticism of capitalism," said Rioux, "but you still hold as valuable the individual. It was a philosophy called personalism."

Domenach described Esprit's philosophy in much the same way, going back to its roots during the depression.

"Capitalism was catastrophic. It was taking the world to war and it wasn't working.

"But state collectivism wouldn't work either," he said, so Mounier followed a middle road, "a little like English labour socialism, but with a Catholic influence."

Domenach said he felt very close to Trudeau politically in those days.

"My ideas were the same as his and his ideas were the same as mine—which is why he was our personal representative in French Canada [in later years]."[3]

The only issue on which Domenach said he didn't agree with Trudeau was nationalism.

Domenach said he believed in a certain kind of nationalism,

but recalled that Trudeau thought nationalism in French Canada would lead to fascism.

Mounier himself went to the core of his philosophy in the last editorial he wrote in Esprit before his death, entitled, "Loyalty".

Domenach, Marrou and Paul Fraisse, who made up Esprit's editorial committee, later made this pledge in a dedication to Mounier. "The loyalty that we owe him is to continue – not to replace or succeed, which is impossible – but to continue Esprit" as outlined in his last editorial, "a sort of testament".

"We have never been," wrote Mounier, "on the main track of the communist party. Our philosophy, which owes some of its health to Marxist waters, has never received its blessing. While it does agree with some of the actual perspectives of Marxism, its fundamentals are different and everything has been modified. If we've paid particular attention to communism in France after 1944, it's because particular conditions in France forced us to. The Resistance left us the promise of a communism re-integrated into the French tradition, capable of being reformed into a French socialism with our new experience and less utopianism . . .

"As long as there was a chance we could shake the French nation awake by a union with the party that more or less represents the productive forces in this country, the French proletariat, we have pushed it."

Mounier admitted that the Communist Party of France imitated and worshipped the Soviet party, that it lied and covered up lies and imposed a rigid discipline on its cadres.

"Is that a childhood illness or an incurable cancer – only the future will tell," said Mounier. "Because it's still largely the party of the proletariat, we'll never join those who fight it with arms. We'll content ourselves with fighting it with the truth."

He said early socialism, Marxism and Leninism had all used violence to achieve their ends as a short term solution. That was too high a price to pay, he thought.

The problem that faced not only socialists but all Frenchmen, said Mounier, was to find out how the end could be reached today in an orderly fashion, and not through deaths.

Mounier set for himself a duty to "avoid with patience, robustness and objective intelligence a rupture between the Communist Party and the rest of the nation.

"We ought to rethink entirely the problem of the non-communist left. The negative conditions are clear: no systematic anti-communism and no labour socialism where one merely draws from several systems.

"It [the proletariat] must be allowed to continue the positive work of the communist party while eliminating all the poisons which are mixed therein. Such is one of our principal tasks for tomorrow. We will emphasize that as much as possible in our review, and our wish is that one day we can work together in such a task with a purified communism."[4]

It had been an eventful year for Trudeau. Before he returned to Canada for the summer he travelled by motorcycle through France and Spain with Andrée Desautels.

Trudeau had a chance to practise the Spanish he had learned under a tutor at his home in Montreal and Desautels recalled that "all along the way he would stop and talk to the people.

"Once he became terribly upset when a labourer told him that a day's work would earn him only enough for a loaf of bread. Another time he found a gasoline attendant who could recite Don Quixote with him. Pierre was delighted with that. Pierre has a universal mind . . . "

Trudeau returned home to find Canadians thoroughly shocked by a Russian named Igor Gouzenko, who had defected from the Soviet embassy in Ottawa where he had worked as a cypher clerk. This had forced the appointment of a Royal Commission of Inquiry.

It hadn't been easy for Gouzenko to defect. First he had had a difficult time finding someone who would accept him and the bundle of top secret documents he had stuffed into his shirt. Then, when he was accepted by the Royal Canadian Mounted Police, Prime Minister MacKenzie King almost handed him back to the Russians. He found Gouzenko a political embarrassment.

Gouzenko's revelations sent several Canadians to jail as spies, among them Fred Rose, who had the distinction of being the only communist ever elected to the House of Commons. Gouzenko's full testimony was never released but he did say the spy ring he exposed in Canada was only one of four.

Trudeau decided to once more pursue his studies and he left for the London School of Economics and Political Science.

London was just picking itself up from the rubble created by the blitz and the later buzz bombs. In fact, part of the LSE was so badly damaged by bombing it was eventually demolished.

But while it was physically battered, its spirits in final victory were high.

About 3,000 students jammed the school during the year 1947-48, many of them ex-servicemen. There were 33 other Canadian students there besides Trudeau, among them Paul Fox, John Porter, Morris Miller, Georges Charpentier, Phillip Garigue and Robert McKenzie.

As a graduate student Trudeau didn't have many regular lectures and because he kept pretty well to himself, other Canadians remember very little about him.

He was one of a handful of students who were under the personal tutorship of Professor Harold Laski, an academic so well-known that his name became virtually synonymous with the LSE.

Laski was in a period of spiritual and physical decline during those years, but his intellect was still intact.

McKenzie remembers Trudeau as "a little rich left-winger – but enormously interesting" and "an intellectual dillettante".

He, John Porter and several other Canadian students were sympathetic to the CCF party in Canada and formed the Canadian Progressive Student Club "with a general left-inclination".

But Trudeau wouldn't have any part of it, said McKenzie. "Trudeau was flirting with Marxism in those days. We Canadians felt that Pierre was to the left of us. He always gave the impression of being bemused at the sombre quality of Canadian leftists."

With his general air and a little MG, "there was always a slight aura of the playboy about him," McKenzie recalled.

Trudeau's year might not have been arduous, but it clearly was formative for him.

He later recalled Professor Harold Laski as "the most stimulating and powerful influence" he encountered.[5]

At various times Laski was an avowed opponent of communism, a supporter of a united front with the communists to oppose Hitler, Mussolini and Franco and finally a Fabian socialist on the left wing of the Labour Party, in which he had been chairman of the national executive.

Trudeau said it was at the LSE that he first became enthused with the British writer, Lord Acton, notably his book "Freedom and Power". He also read Laski's own work, the "Grammar of Politics".

Laski's central principles, as he described them, were: "the necessarily federal character of society; the incompatibility of the sovereign state with that economic world order so painfully struggling to be born; the antithesis between individual property rights in the essential means of production and the fulfilment of the democratic idea; the thesis that liberty is a concept devoid of real meaning except in the context of equality . . .

"There cannot, in a word, be democracy unless there is socialism . . . capitalism in distress makes impossible the effective operation of international institutions . . . Capitalism, in a word, is rooted in a system which makes power the criterion of right and war the ultimate expression of power."

In another book, "Parliamentary Government in England," Laski described the essence of Fabian socialism as: the repudiation of the Marxist doctrine of class war; the belief that "there was no way to power save through the ballot box" and the "permeation of existing political parties rather than the creation of a separate political party".[6]

This philosophy obviously had a great influence on Trudeau. Several of his friends would describe him not long after his year at the LSE as a "Fabian socialist".

"For Trudeau the British labour movement had the greatest impact – the Fabian socialism of the first half-century. It was very influential on his political evolution," said his friend from Paris, Jean-Marc Léger.

Trudeau, McKenzie and others sometimes signed up for special weekly meetings at Laski's house in Fulham. It was a way of informally gathering a wide cross-section of the left-wing of London at the time.

While Trudeau and his friends were enjoying the fruits of peace after six years of war, there was another war developing. This new war would be fought quietly, covertly and for the most part, without weapons. It was called the "Cold War".

In the first three post-war years, Russia gobbled up several small Baltic states, staged a coup in Czechoslovakia, installed communist regimes in Poland, Rumania, Bulgaria and Hungary and was fomenting revolt in Greece.

Germany was divided, tension was high, and it threatened to become a flashpoint. To counter Soviet expansion the allies formed the North Atlantic Treaty Organization and the U.S. poured billions of dollars into the 19 countries covered under the Marshall Plan.

Elsewhere in the world there was chaos. Moslem Pakistan had become independent of Hindu India and a religious war erupted with blood-curdling massacres.

The French were embroiled in a costly conflict with the communist-backed Viet Minh in Indo-China, while farther to the north in China Mao Tse-tung was fighting a vast war with Chiang Kai-shek.

It was around this tumultuous world that Trudeau decided to travel in the spring of 1948.

His friend Gerard Pelletier said later that Trudeau believed that the more a traveller spent on a hotel the less he got to know the people.

Trudeau certainly seemed to believe it then. He set off in May on an eleven-month trip which he later claimed cost him only $800. With him were two others from the LSE, Morris Miller and K. R. Narayanan.

He presented a rather unconventional picture in those days: a 29-year-old with stubbly blond beard, army jungle hat, shorts and a rucksack on his back.

The details of the odyssey's first leg through Europe are confused and contradictory. While it's clear Trudeau visited Poland, Czechoslovakia, Austria, Germany, Hungary and Yugoslavia, it's far from clear in what order they were visited, and under what circumstances.

Trudeau himself was quoted as saying much of his travelling was done at the expense of communists and their organizations. "It was in the days when they were courting students. You could live off the fat of the land," he was quoted as saying.[7]

Another account described a similar arrangement. "He signed on as a French-English interpreter for a free trip to a trade fair in Poland with the communist International Union of Students." The same account quoted Trudeau as saying "in those days the communists did anything for students".[8]

But Miller said he didn't remember Trudeau working as an interpreter for the IUS and was generally reluctant to talk about the trip, although he did supply a few details.

He and Trudeau travelled first to Germany before crossing into Austria, where they had to bluff their way past border guards as they didn't have any visas.

"We took some Labour Party stationery and typed out a message saying 'let the bearer pass without hindrance etc.' The officials just wanted to see something official," Miller said.

"Going into Vienna – it was occupied by the four powers – we slept on the train covered by coats hoping no one would disturb us and they didn't."

Vienna was then worse off than either London or Paris.

"I can remember Austrians looking into bakeshop windows. They were quite hard up," he said. The two of them visited a rest camp for refugees from the concentration camps.

"Trudeau was fascinated – we went there quite a few times. It was interesting, I would ask some question in Yiddish but they would answer to him. Pierre said he looked more Jewish than I did."

The two then travelled to Prague with Narayanan, whom Miller described as "small and very dark-skinned".

"Pierre put on a tam and ground sheet and I put on an army coat. We formed his bodyguard—he looked like a real Mafia type. We went into some nightclubs and got a great laugh wherever we went."

From there he and Trudeau went in late August to Warsaw,

devastated by a battle between the Nazis and a handful of heroic Jews in the ghetto, by a battle between the Russians and the Nazis for control of the city and finally by the cold-blooded, methodical demolition of many major buildings by the Nazis before they left the city.

"We were terribly impressed by the ruins," Miller recalled. "At that time it was destroyed, all the buildings were gutted. He got a first-hand view of what the hell war could do."

The two then met Steven Endicott and Norman Nerenberg, from Toronto and Montreal, who were leaders of a group of youthful, left-wing Canadians called the Beaver Brigade which was helping to rebuild eastern Europe.

Nerenberg viewed the ghetto as a "testimonial to the bestiality of the Nazis and an example of what will happen if the mad millionaires of Wall Street have their way now".

Shortly before, Endicott had been awarded the "gold shock workers' medal" for helping to rebuild Lidice in Czechoslovakia and he and Nerenberg were in Warsaw to attend the International Young Workers Conference as delegates.

Nerenberg recalls Trudeau as a "quiet spoken, retiring individual" and met him again later in Otwock, near Warsaw at another conference. This was the World Council meeting of the World Federation of Democratic Youth, a communist front organization. Nerenberg was a delegate to it as he was a member of the National Labour Youth Federation, the youth wing of the Labour Progressive Party of Canada.

He remembers Trudeau and Miller attending the Council meeting as observers.

From Warsaw they made their way to Budapest, Hungary, in the first week of August, where the communists had organized a trade fair for the east European countries. Miller said they visited the fair and "met a woman in a booth who thought we should meet some local girls. So we came back an hour later and she had a couple of attractive Magyar girls there. We took them out but Pierre didn't think they were as attractive as French girls.

"That changed, though, when we went to an open air performance of Die Fledermaus and we looked around at all the gorgeous girls and Pierre said 'well ... O.K.'"

Trudeau then bumped into a university student from Toronto, William Kilbourn. Kilbourn recalls that Trudeau talked about a job with the privy council office in Ottawa at the time "as if it was a definite thing. He had some kind of arrangement to get back to."

Before he did, however, Trudeau was "quite keen to get into Yugoslavia," Kilbourn said.

It was in Budapest that Trudeau and Miller split up and Trudeau continued south to Yugoslavia, one of the most devastated countries in Europe.

Before the war, the country was poor but relatively peaceful. During the Nazi occupation, two resistance factions bid for Allied support. One faction was led by Draja Mikhailovich and was backed by the country's monarchy, the other was led by Josip Broz, a communist whose nom de guerre was Tito.

For every German killed by the resistance, 10 innocent Yugoslavs were murdered. When the end of the war came the two factions fought each other briefly until Tito won after finally hunting down Mikhailovich.

Tito was in the unenviable position of being hated by the Soviets, from whom he had just declared independence, and suspected by the Allies because he was a communist.

The borders to the country were tightly sealed, so tightly in fact, that about the time Trudeau visited the country two high state officials were killed trying to cross it.

There were reported cases of starvation and widespread malnutrition outside major centres. A black market in essential goods was booming.

The Yugoslavs had mounted a tremendous effort to rebuild railways and bombed-out buildings, but the products were more the result of eagerness to get the jobs done and excessive thriftiness than solid construction.

Trudeau continued on to Bulgaria, where he hitched up with some gypsies who were Sephardic Jews and travelled through Greece to the frontier of Europe where he swam the Bosphorus to Turkey.

"It wasn't that hard, but it was cold and had a bloody strong current," he recalled.

From there he made his way through Syria and Lebanon until he reached Amman, Jordan. He dropped into the Philadelphia Hotel to find some journalists, who were covering the Israeli-Arab conflict, holding up the bar.

Israel had declared independence in May only to be attacked within days by Egypt, Syria, Jordan, Iraq and Lebanon. The Israelis survived, barely, to fight again and again.

It was about mid-September and the journalists told him it was impossible to visit Jerusalem. But he managed to get a lift on a truck of Arab irregulars heading for the front in the city and within hours of his arrival there was thrown into jail as a suspected spy. Count Bernadotte, the United Nations envoy, had been assassinated, and feelings were running high.

He was soon released and took in Ur of the Chaldees and the pyramids before making his way to the Indian subcontinent. Trudeau walked through the Khyber Pass, tasted goats' milk and wild honey and watched the Afghans collect a toll from travellers entering the pass.

Pakistan was next, then in the throes of a war with India, where he met a railway engineer in Lahore and stayed with him and his family for a few days, learning the local customs.

Skirting Nepal he passed through Lucknow and arrived in what is now Bangladesh shortly before Christmas, 1948. He stayed for a week or two and met some of the Holy Cross Fathers stationed as missionaries there.

Father Guy Tourangeau, a member of the order, was in Barisal at the time and remembers that Trudeau didn't exactly get the red carpet treatment.

"At that time the police were looking for a cheque forger. Finding Mr. Trudeau landing from the steamer, in army boots, corduroy pants, long beard and a haversack they said, 'that's our man!' and took him immediately before a magistrate ... on suspicion of a criminal offence.

"When the magistrate discovered the mistake, he apologized and offered him a chair and some tea while he sent word to the parish nearby. . . .

"However, he was directed to report to the police before leaving Chittagong for Burma. Of course Pierre 'forgot' com-

34

pletely, with the result that the secret police were at my place in Barisal, about one month afterwards, asking about him.

"Nobody ever knew why he had been requested to report to the police before leaving the country . . . at that time and until 1958, Canadians were not aliens in the country."

After Trudeau had visited several missionaries at various centres, he set off through Burma, then seething with a vicious civil war. He then moved down through Indo-China, visiting Thailand, Cambodia – where he saw the fabled ancient city of Angkor Wat – and Vietnam, where the French were fighting. Finally, on a truck full of bound and gagged prisoners, he headed for Saigon in a convoy.

After taking a ship to Hong Kong he entered Nationalist China on a visa he had obtained in Ankara, Turkey.

Chiang Kai-shek and his army had their backs to the wall then. Trudeau passed through Canton, where he visited the Isle of Sha-mun, an exclusive enclave for foreigners and diplomatic representatives, and off limits to Chinese. He also visited some opium dens which had somehow survived a clampdown by Chiang.

From there he headed north to Shanghai to find the city in chaos. Mao's troops were across the Yangtze River and no one knew how long the Nationalists could hold out.

Trudeau sailed from Shanghai only five days before the city fell.

By late March he had left the pain and violence of civil war, revolution, famine and disease far behind as he touched shore back in Canada, a tranquil, rational corner in a world that seemed to have gone mad.

FOOTNOTES CHAPTER 3

1. Quartier Latin, October 14, 1957.
2. Trudeau to the University of Montreal's International Relations Club, September 22, 1947.

3. From an interview with the author, in Paris, October 12, 1977.
4. Esprit, February, 1950.
5. Weekend Magazine, No. 13, 1966.
6. Harold Laski, "Parliamentary Government in England," George Allen and Unwin Ltd., London, 1938.
7. Toronto Telegram, April 2, 1968.
8. Martin Sullivan, "Mandate '68", Doubleday Canada Ltd., Toronto, 1968.

4

Getting Involved

The old law school classmate of Trudeau's father, Maurice Lenoblet Duplessis had good reason to feel smug in the early spring of 1949.

Less than a year before, on July 28, he had led his National Union party in Quebec to a staggering victory, capturing 82 of 92 seats in the legislature.

The Roman Catholic church was left to exert its powerful influence in the union movement, co-operative societies and education with the blessing of Duplessis.

Duplessis' party had been created in the early thirties from the union of a conservative and a nationalist party.

Twenty years later, the province could be accurately described as being nationalist and conservative in sentiment, with large doses of authoritarianism and deep religious conviction thrown in.

Duplessis, his party, and part of the church clergy, stood for the very things Trudeau detested.

He was not quite alone. There were a handful of other individuals who were outspoken in their opposition to Duplessis.

At Laval University in Quebec City the Dean of the Faculty of Social Sciences was the Dominican priest Father Georges-Henri Lévesque. One of Lévesque's students, Maurice Lamontagne, headed the department of economy.

Both Lévesque and Lamontagne agitated for change, but they

were vulnerable as the faculty was funded by a provincial government grant. Duplessis was shortly to cut off the funding for its opposition to his regime.

Duplessis was an ardent anti-communist and during his first term in power, in 1937, had enacted the Padlock Law, which allowed provincial police to raid any premises and seize propaganda supporting the communist cause. After the seizure the premises could be padlocked. Although it was only applied about a dozen times in its 20-year existence, it was an affront to left-wingers and civil libertarians in the province.

"Le Chef," as Duplessis was called, tended to identify his most virulent opposition with communists. He called Father Lévesque and his faculty "those communists" and dismissed the editors and writers at Quebec's most influential French-language daily, Le Devoir, as "those Bolsheviks".

Another area of opposition to Duplessis was found within the union movement. While it was still dominated by the church, there were militants like Jean Marchand who became the provincial organizer for the Catholic Labour Confederation of Canada in 1944, who were also working for a change.

Then there was the Jeunesse Étudiante Catholique, the youth wing of the church organization, Action Catholique. Gerard Pelletier and others worked actively there to promote change, and frequently courted official church condemnation for doing it.

Politically, there was very little real opposition to Duplessis even though 40 per cent of the province had voted against him in 1948. The socialist CCF was seen by most Quebecers as an extreme left-wing, English Canadian party.

The Liberal Party in Quebec was in a state of disarray after its 1948 defeat. Within it there were large elements of both the old guard who had presided over the electoral disaster and left-wing, young Turks such as Jean-Louis Gagnon.

By 1944 Gagnon had stopped identifying publicly with the Labour Progressive Party, as the Communist Party of Canada was then known, and started supporting the Liberals.

He later explained, "I stopped believing in socialism when I discovered the reality of the USSR, the failure of the system, after the war." Gagnon didn't see the move to the Liberal Party as a radical move.

"What does it mean to be a Liberal? Nothing precise – for me it meant being part of a certain progress, of change when it was possible."[1]

He had met Hector Langevin, an old friend of Jean-Charles Emile Trudeau who, Gagnon said, acted as an "informal guardian" for the younger Trudeau at times.

Langevin was the well-to-do owner of Valiquette Ltd., a Montreal furniture store, and active backer for the Liberal Party. He bankrolled a series of 15-minute radio broadcasts Gagnon gave for the Liberals during their '44 election campaign.

Gagnon recalls meeting Trudeau one Sunday for lunch at Langevin's big house in Ste. Adèle, near Montreal, in the spring of 1949.

"Pierre was not a Liberal, he was quite a radical. He was fresh out of the London School of Economics and a Fabian socialist. I tried several times to bring him into the Liberal Party but he wouldn't join."

Trudeau shared the opinion of his friend, Pelletier, that the Liberals were scarcely any better than Duplessis' National Union.

Gagnon's influence in the Liberal Party grew until, when Georges-Henri Lapalme was elected provincial Liberal leader in 1950, he said he became the "éminence grise" behind Lapalme.

Gagnon met Pelletier during a public affairs conference that year in Couchiching, Ontario and tried to recruit him into the party, but Pelletier wouldn't have any of it.

"Your party isn't a democratic party – there is no structure, you just have a chief," Gagnon said Pelletier told him.

This prompted Gagnon to work on a brief with Pelletier suggesting ways to democratize the party, which eventually resulted in the Quebec Liberal Federation.

But, exasperatingly, "he still wouldn't join the Liberals. He and Trudeau were still to the left of the Liberals."

Another friend recalled that although Trudeau refused to join the CCF, he supported it actively soon after his return to Canada.

"I received a call at about eleven one night from Pierre, who was at the CCF headquarters. He said, 'I see you haven't got your membership card – I want your five dollars and you'll receive your card in a week.' "

The friend immediately went out, had a terrible photograph taken for the membership card and dutifully sent it in with his five dollars. About a week later he bumped into Trudeau, told him what a terrible photo he had, and asked to see his.

"I don't have a card," Trudeau told him. "I tell you, the day I enter politics it will be with the Liberals. I don't want to be a missionary all my life. When I enter politics it will be to do something."

Deciding "what to do" was a real problem for the fragmented, miniscule centres of opposition to Duplessis until a strike at Asbestos literally exploded on the Quebec scene.

Asbestos was a small town on the south side of the St. Lawrence River, near the U.S. border where the Johns-Manville Company had a large asbestos mine worked by about 2,000 men.

They were members of a union affiliated to the CLCC and Jean Marchand, secretary-general of the Confederation, had travelled there to help handle the negotiation of a new contract.

A devastating series of articles in Le Devoir by an American 18 months earlier had strongly linked asbestos to a fatal lung disease and caused an uproar.

At issue were these demands: an 18 per cent wage increase (from 85¢ to one dollar an hour); a union-supervised pension plan; union approval of promotions, transfers and dismissals; the right to discuss production standards and improved health standards.

In 1949, these were radical demands and the company largely refused them. In mid-February, Marchand appealed to the workers for a few more days to make a final appeal to the province to help settle the deadlock, but the irate miners voted to go on strike illegally.

They were soon supported by others working in a mine at nearby Thetford run by Andrew Johnson's Company.

At first, it was just another strike. Then, in the early hours of

March 26, the back yard of Andrew Johnson, president of the Thetford mine, was dynamited. At Asbestos, a railway spur line was blown up and emotions ran high.

One hundred provincial police were rushed into Asbestos and a confrontation seemed imminent.

Support for the striking miners was quickly mobilized.

A group called the Équipe de Recherches Sociales at the University of Montreal started collecting money for the strikers under the direction of their secretary, Jean-Marc Léger, Trudeau's friend from his Paris days. Active in the Équipe were three men at Le Devoir: Pelletier, who was covering the strike; André Laurendeau, the paper's editor-in-chief and Gerard Filion, an editor. Le Devoir itself backed the union strongly.

At Laval University another collection was taken up by students in the social science faculty of Father Lévesque. Lamontagne was also involved in the effort and said the students were told by the university's rector not to travel to Asbestos to present the money as they had intended or they would be expelled.

Lamontagne, feeling more secure, took the students off the hook and delivered the funds himself.

Archbishop Joseph Charbonneau of Montreal allowed union posters soliciting strike funds to be hung in his diocese and more than $167,000 was raised. Although he was supported by Archbishop Maurice Roy in Quebec City, he was generally considered an outsider by the Quebec clergy, as he was French Canadian from Manitoba and sympathetic to the socialist CCF.

His involvement caused him to resign less than a year later after he was attacked by some members of the church hierarchy.

Johns-Manville had taken a hard line. It took out full page advertisements in major newspapers attacking the strike as illegal and unwarranted, began hiring scabs and evicted strikers from their company houses.

Pelletier had been covering the strike from the beginning. When he was driving from Montreal to Asbestos one day he picked up Michel Chartrand, his friend from Jeunesse Étudiante Catholique in earlier days, and persuaded him to come along to see the action.

Chartrand found some action all right. Within days he was thrown in jail and remained involved with union work for the next 28 years.

On April 22 Pelletier gave Trudeau a lift to Asbestos. Trudeau's first day in Asbestos was one to remember.

Pelletier's British, right-hand drive car was stopped by the first policeman they encountered, who walked over to Trudeau, sitting where the driver usually would, and asked to see his driver's license. Trudeau had a short beard, and wore jeans, shirt, old jacket, and a tattered raincoat.

He didn't have a license and the two were hauled into the Iroquois Club which the police were using as their operations centre. The mistake was soon discovered, much to the embarrassment of the police, and they were released.

That evening, Pelletier took Trudeau to the Ste. Aimé Church hall where he met Jean Marchand for the first time. Marchand invited him to speak to a meeting of miners on the legal aspects of the strike and Trudeau gladly obliged.

It was not the kind of speech he had anticipated, he said.

"Miners are not schoolchildren, you know, and while students might steal pencils, the miners steal dynamite. They use it all day at work, and they are familiar with it. Now, I had managed to defuse two or three cute little plots by the boys which would have blown up the mine manager and most of his staff.

"So you can imagine that when Trudeau urged physical resistance by the strikers, I got a little bit worried."[2]

Marchand managed to keep a lid on the miners' anger and their spirits up at the same time. Support for the strike was growing daily until on May 1 it reached its peak with a sermon on the strike and its importance by Archbishop Charbonneau in Montreal's Notre Dame Cathedral.

"There's a conspiracy to destroy the working class, and it's the church's duty to intervene," he declared.

Only days later, Duplessis himself intervened when hundreds more provincial police, armed with truncheons and submachineguns, were bussed into Asbestos after the strikers had overturned and burned several cars.

The Riot Act was read and 180 people were arrested. Of

those, about 100 were released the same day, while scores of others were detained and interrogated.

Trudeau was in the thick of it, marching in picket lines and talking to strikers. A week after the Riot Act was read Jean-Paul Geoffroy, a strike director, recalled Trudeau spoke at another union meeting.

"They were a little worried about Trudeau", said Geoffroy. The strikers suspected the police were monitoring them through the use of informants and outside spies. To allay their suspicions, Geoffroy invited Trudeau to speak to them.

"So Trudeau spoke about the names given to police in all the countries he had visited – in France they were called 'cows.' They all laughed."

The strike wound down and after a compromise was worked out it was sent to arbitration.

The conflict was to have a lasting effect on Quebec and the individuals involved. Pelletier went into union work with the CLCC and although Trudeau refused a job with them, he often acted as counsel for them in later years. Geoffroy says he helped gather evidence to defend several miners who had been charged during the strike.

For Quebec as a whole, the strike produced two profound results. Duplessis' will had not been done, and a deep division had appeared in church ranks over social questions.

The summer of 1949 passed quickly and on September 7 Trudeau found himself doing what he had considered with Kilbourn in Budapest the year before when he joined the privy council office. This was less than a month before he turned thirty. He had been toying with the idea of joining the department of finance. Robert Bryce, then secretary to the treasury board and assistant deputy minister in the department, interviewed him for the position, but he finally decided on the privy council office instead.

He was taken on as a grade one officer at an annual salary of $2,880. It must have been a novel, if somewhat boring experience for Trudeau after his global adventures only months old. Senior civil servants are notoriously colourless, apolitical (at least publicly) and discreet. He had gone a long way from urging strikers to physical resistance, to a nine to five job where he was expected to accomplish such demanding tasks as listing the number of federal-provincial agreements within a certain period.

Nevertheless, he settled into an apartment on King Edward Street in Ottawa with Jean Gelinas, an old friend from his Jean de Brébeuf days and applied himself to his job.

While he was finding his way about Ottawa's corridors of power some of his friends in Montreal began meeting in informal study groups to discuss Quebec society.

Reginald Boisvert, who was to become the Quebec secretary of the socialist CCF party, recalls the group was centred around Guy Cormier and two old hands from the Jeunesse Étudiante Catholique, Pelletier and Pierre Juneau.

"We were trying to shape up opinions on the general situation in Quebec. The aim at that time was to put out a publication and Trudeau came in shortly afterwards," he said. At the time Juneau was working in the National Film Board in Ottawa and Pelletier was becoming involved with the CLCC.

"The JEC group was very much interested in Emmanuel Mounier's 'Catholics of the Left' movement," Boisvert said. "It evolved that most of the people got involved in politics and social questions. We came very near to being condemned a few times. We were taking positions the church didn't like."

While Trudeau had to spend Monday to Friday tied to Ottawa he regularly escaped to Montreal on the weekends to the discussion groups and he wrote to Roger Rolland in Vancouver about the developments. Rolland soon joined the group with Maurice Blain, Jean-Paul Geoffroy, Charles Lussier and Marcel Rioux.

One of the group's members said their common ground was that "we were all interested in the CCF and the unions . . . and were all socialist minded and adamantly against Duplessis.

"We were anti-clerical (against the official church's clergy) but in the right sense. We were all devout Catholics." He said the group opposed the church's extensive influence in education and health and its great land holdings.

The group also opposed, of course, "parochial nationalism".

Not all of the group were devout Catholics, though. Marcel Rioux, an atheist, remembers telling Trudeau "we can go a long way together but when Duplessis is out, I go my own route".

In the early spring of 1950 the group had firmed up its ideas for a publication and held a meeting in the summer house rented jointly by the Pelletier and Geoffroy families on Île Perrot.

Geoffroy thought up the name Cité Libre for the magazine and they settled on a format.

"Esprit was the paragon – the model – of Cité Libre," recalled Rioux. Boisvert said "it was a very special kind of magazine group. Everyone had a say about everything and the first issue took about half a year to put out."

While the editorial office would be listed at 84 McCulloch Street – Trudeau's home – some of the meetings took place in Lussier's basement with a gallon jug of red wine and some cheese. Each contributor would read his article openly and be criticized. Finally the article would be hammered into shape collectively. So, in a sense, each article that appeared was written by them all.

Each member put in $25, a printer was found, articles were written and the first copy came off the press in June, 1950, the same month as the start of the Korean war.

The city of Montreal was divided into sections and each Cité Libriste took an armful of issues out to persuade bookstores to stock and sell them.

The magazine's first editorial laid out clearly the reason for its existence and to whom it was directed.

"For some years, hundreds of us have suffered in silence; and that's why Cité Libre comes to you today . . . We have something to say.

"Each of our articles will be an invitation to those, aged thirty or less, who haven't said anything yet, and those who have had the chance, but who haven't been able to speak from the bottom of their hearts."

Cité Libre also wanted to be a rallying point for thought and action among people separated by space and profession, action that would be "modest, threatened, but resolute".

Trudeau's first contribution was entitled "On Functional Politics". The word "functional" was to recur again and again in his writings in one form or another.

He wanted to start with the fundamentals: that there were Christian and French facts in North America. The rest was open to questioning and analysis.

Trudeau also wanted to get rid of the emotion-charged vocabulary of Quebec politics. "Coldly, let's be intelligent," he wrote.

One word that often raised passions was "autonomy" for Quebec, he said. "It's not an idea, it's a warcry."

But "inescapable historical necessities" were quietly forcing a process of centralization upon Canada and the world, said Trudeau.

"Nowhere does power not tend to grow: it's a universal law, and why should Ottawa be the exception?... But there's more. In these days, fiscal and economic theory both support the necessity of centralization... Monetary and banking theory are also leading us in this direction... the theory behind the union movement gives us compelling reasons for centralization... all the ideological thrusts are for centralization, for a union."

Trudeau was tearing apart one of Quebec's "great truths," but he persisted.

"After that, can you really say autonomy is good and centralization is bad?... Don't we have to stop being for or against, and start worrying about establishing positions a little more surely that can put us back on history's track?"

After questioning and then condemning some aspects of autonomy for Quebec, he mentioned that he foresaw a profound study on a definite separation of the Church and the State.

In five pages, Trudeau had gone after two of the basic power structures in Quebec and the glue that held them together. He was signalling the opening of a war of wits with Duplessis and the official church hierarchy.

Cité Libre's first issue had promised the magazine would appear every three months, but it wasn't until February, 1951, that the next issue appeared. There was a good reason for the seven months' delay.

Readers had swamped Cité Libre with letters saying that

while its arguments were illuminating, they were too short, incomplete and generally insufficient.

Pelletier was set the task of responding to the letters and he did so in an article called "Cité Libre Confesses Its Intentions".

He gave the general background of the magazine and its contributors and observed that French Canadian youth were rebelling against accepted values and ideas.

"Five years ago, we said 'Capitalism is dead, it's an out-of-date system.' We dreamed of unity among the labour unions and we wanted to get rid of their religious affiliation.

"Five years later ... are we getting ready to turn the clock back? Surely not."

The first task that the Cité Libristes had set themselves, said Pelletier, was to outline problem areas and decide on plans of action.

Trudeau continued his examination of what he called "functional politics" by responding to some readers who had concluded from his first article that he was a centralizer.

He defended a certain amount of provincial autonomy by predicting that limitless, centralized power would result in "the servant of the people" becoming a despot. Aside from that, Trudeau didn't think it would be possible for one central government to handle all of Canada's diverse problems, and even went so far as to quote Maurice Duplessis to back him up.

A balance of power between the two levels of bureaucracy must be achieved before the nation could achieve good government, said Trudeau. One other factor needed for competent government was involvement in the democratic process by each citizen, he added.

"A state where citizens don't interest themselves in politics is destined to slavery," he wrote.

"There are no divine rights for either prime ministers or priests: they don't have any authority over us that we don't want them to have. Once we understand these truths, we will have stopped being a 'young people ... ' "

As long as Trudeau applied himself to problems related to Quebec society, he didn't risk any conflict with his employers in Ottawa. But during 1951, after Canada had committed troops to

Korea to fight a communist invasion across the 38th parallel, Trudeau rankled at the government's stand on the war and opposed Prime Minister Louis St. Laurent's support of it.

Michel Chartrand, Trudeau's old associate in the League for the Defence of Canada in 1942, remembers meeting him at Pelletier's home on July 14 at a party to celebrate France's Bastille Day.

"Louis St. Laurent is talking peace but planning war," Trudeau said, according to Chartrand.

Only two months earlier Cité Libre had printed an editorial opposing the war that strongly bore the imprint of Trudeau.

The 11-page editorial judged that while the invasion by the North Korean communists constituted an injustice, the response by the United Nations was so disproportionate that it was an injustice greater than the one they were trying to remedy.

It also condemned the facts that Korea had been divided by the great powers along the 38th parallel and that a "corrupt, reactionary" government with "aggressive designs on North Korea" was installed in the south.

"The United States can't forgive the Chinese people for chasing out the Kuomintang [Chiang Kai-shek's nationalist forces], whose shameful corruption wasn't at all incompatible with international high finance."

This was why, said Cité Libre, an offensive was launched to reach China's borders, why the borders were violated and China was condemned as an aggressor in the U.N.

The U.N. intervened because "western countries, above all the U.S., feared that Asia would develop outside the capitalist orbit.

"It's impossible to believe that the lightning war unleashed by the North Koreans and the subsequent reunification of the whole of Korea under a government, even communist, atheist or totalitarian, would have been able to produce as many collective injustices . . . as those which resulted from the military intervention by the United Nations."

The U.S. was only interested in seeing "liberated nations become American-style democracies, that's to say, respectful of free enterprise and private property. Thus, they contributed almost everywhere to the protection of the most reactionary feudalism and didn't see that capitalism is a meaningless formula for countries of 80 per cent illiteracy and where the average annual income is less than $40 per capita.

"Because Marxists have always been the first ones to proclaim the urgency of liberating colonial regimes, the Americans have always feared that the Kremlin was behind Asian nationalism. . . .

"The Americans are incapable of imagining that socialist, and even communist, countries can become anti-Stalinist forces: thus they refuse to recognize the government of 400 million Chinese, and oblige it to remain in the Soviet orbit."

Cité Libre then moved to direct criticism of Canadian government actions, which must have put Trudeau, by now one of the two editors of the magazine, in a difficult position in the privy council office.

"The speech of our minister of external affairs [Lester Bowles Pearson], given in the House of Commons . . . has to be read to understand how pathetic it is to see clearsightedness in the service of cowardice."

Pearson was quoted as saying that although he found it "premature and unwise" to condemn China as an aggressor in Korea, Canada had done so in the U.N. to preserve western unity on the issue.

"Great God! Are we to renounce forever the hope of seeing a public, Canadian man, standing on his hind feet, act on his own?"

Trudeau resigned from the privy council office October 28, 1951. He never revealed why he quit his first steady job, whether from boredom, revulsion over the government's Korean stand or simply wanderlust.

It may have been the latter, for shortly afterward he began a fateful trip to Europe which took him to Moscow, a trip which would raise a storm of controversy in Quebec and haunt him 25 years later.

FOOTNOTES CHAPTER 4

1. La Presse, June 22, 1976.
2. Martin Sullivan, Op. Cit.

5

Moscow

By 1950 the Soviet Union was in trouble.

It had barely survived the devastation and butchery of the German onslaught by fighting a grim rearguard, leaving a burnt wasteland behind it, devoid of food, machinery and people.

With fanatical determination it hung on while the western allies poured arms and food into Stalin's Russia to sustain the front. As the tide turned, Stalin's intentions became all too clear.

As his troops neared Warsaw, in Poland, the underground began a heroic fight to help the Russians liberate their city. But Stalin gave his orders, and his troops waited patiently until the Germans crushed the last vestiges of Polish resistance before taking the city. Stalin didn't want anyone who knew how to resist tyranny to exist in the Poland he envisioned.

With the war's end, eastern Europe fell under the viselike grip of Stalin, whose name fittingly translates as "steel".

Churchill's "Iron Curtain" sprang from the European soil and lines hardened. Hundreds of thousands of Russian soldiers, liberated from their German captors, were shamefully repatriated by the West against their will. They were promptly marched into a series of Russian concentration camps which would be known years later as the Gulag Archipelago.

These men had committed the sin of being "tainted" by the West in German camps. There were others who had served against the Germans who were deemed to be similarly tainted. They, too, were interned.

Seven years after the war's end, in 1952, it was estimated there were between eight and 13.5 million slave labourers in Russia.[1]

While western nations forged the North Atlantic Treaty Organization, Russia engineered the Warsaw Pact and began building up its arsenal and armed forces.

For a country virtually bled white by the war and deprived of so many young men who languished in the camps, the build-up was a tremendous strain.

Russia was particularly short of strategic materials, which the West had informally agreed not to sell it. Then, as an added incentive not to export those materials, the U.S. passed the Battle Act, which provided that all U.S. economic and military aid to a western country would be cut off if it exported strategic goods to Russia.

In 1951, the U.S. had sold a mere $55,000 worth of goods to Russia, and Stalin was feeling the pinch. He responded with a plan which, it was hoped, would accomplish two ends simultaneously: create disunity among the NATO countries over the question of trade with Russia and obtain strategic materials.

Through the Soviets' largest and most successful front organization, the World Peace Council, a world economic conference was proposed during a meeting in East Berlin, in February, 1951. Another front organization, the World Federation of Trade Unions, also became involved in the plan.

The conference was proposed despite the fact that Russia had permanent purchasing offices in Europe, that the U.N., through its economic, social and cultural commission, could have done it, and that it had been invited by the Economic Commission of Europe to discuss increased trade.

The real purpose of the conference became clear when Louis Saillant, the French general-secretary of the World Federation of Trade Unions, said its aim was to "free many countries in the West from U.S. financial despotism".

A month before Saillant's explanation, in October, 1951, a group calling itself the International Initiating Committee met in the Beaulieu Hotel, Springforbi, Denmark, to plan the conference.

It announced the conference would begin the following April, and would be held in Moscow, as Russia was the only country which had promised that no one would be refused visas.

Invitations were sent to leading businessmen, academics and trade unionists, but most were turned down. Of 200 sent to Americans, only five were accepted. It was the same story in Canada, where again only five accepted. A Toronto newspaper, the Financial Post, was invited but declined while speculating that the conference put Stalin in a difficult position. "From one side of his face he spits hatred of the West. From the other drip honeyed words of courtship."[2]

The style of that prose summed up the unofficial reaction to the conference. Officially, and publicly, the Canadian government didn't take a stand, but instead circulated a document internally urging government employees not to attend.

The Americans didn't bother to hide their feelings about the conference or what they saw as the reasons for it.

"The true purposes of the organizers of this Conference are to confuse and weaken our unity of purpose. They wish to organize pressures in non-communist countries against current restrictions on the export of strategic materials to the Soviet Bloc."

The U.S. state department bulletin went on, "They wish also to discourage us from carrying forward our program of creating strength, strength which is indispensable to maintaining our independence, indispensable to maintaining peace itself."[3]

When it became clear that many of those invited weren't going to attend, Robert Chambeiron, head of the initiating committee in Denmark, sent another member, Pierre Lebrun, on a mission to drum up support through Mexico and Canada.

He held a press conference in Montreal, March 10, but according to one report, while he read out "several high minded conference objectives" he said "he wasn't authorized to say who Canada's delegates might be".[4]

He said the names would be announced in a week after they had been picked by a Canadian committee, whose members would remain nameless. Lebrun was pushed and pushed until he introduced a man sitting beside him, named I. M. Ellenson, who would consider any possible delegates to the conference.

The Canadian delegates who eventually attended were: Marcus Leslie Hancock, a nurseryman who was a member of the Communist Party of Canada; William Garth Teeple, another Party member and manager of the Workers' Co-operative of New Ontario, based in Timmins, Ontario; Michael Freeman (his wife went with him), manager of a co-operative bakery and instructor with the Toronto Labour College, a communist school; Jack Cowan, owner of a travel service and a member of the United Jewish Peoples' Order, a Party front organization; Morris Miller, Trudeau's old friend from the LSE and his world trip, who was listed as an importer-exporter and Trudeau himself, who was officially described as a correspondent for Le Devoir.

In the conference report printed afterwards, Trudeau's name is listed first in the Canadian delegation. While no delegations had designated leaders, a perusal of other countries clearly shows that the most important member of the delegation is listed first.

Canadian delegates are vague about how they were invited to the conference. Hancock says he and the others were invited by a Toronto official of the Party, Leslie Morris. But Freeman and Cowan couldn't remember who invited them and Miller said "some friends at McGill" invited him.

Trudeau was in Europe when Lebrun was making his rounds and later wrote that he received his invitation from the temporary conference headquarters in Denmark. He decided to travel to Moscow by train from Paris, instead of flying via Prague like other delegates.[5]

So he travelled through Austria as far as the end of the American sector at Linz, where the train stopped. He still had to cross 100 miles of the Soviet sector, which the American, British and French soldiers on duty told him was impossible. Nevertheless he crossed the Danube River into the Soviet sector and spoke to a Russian soldier, who took him to a local command post, where all was soon arranged.

He boarded another train and arrived in Prague at 3 a.m. where he was met at the station, fed, given a night's lodging, a Soviet visa and sped on his way the next day with "exemplary courtesy".

He arrived in Moscow Sunday, March 30, four days before the

conference was due to start, but was received "with open arms" nonetheless and installed in the Sovietskaya Hotel, which he called "a masterpiece of vulgarity". Most of the delegates had three-piece suites consisting of a huge living-room with combination radio-television set and upright piano, a bedroom with two outsized twin beds pushed together, tapestries and a balcony, and a library with two telephones and a well-equipped writing desk.

Trudeau settled in and was offered an interpreter and a chauffeured Zis car, which he said closely resembled a luxury Chrysler. But he said he perturbed his hosts somewhat when he asked instead for a map of Moscow and stated his preference for lone walks. He went to Mass on Easter Sunday in Moscow, and continued going for each of the other three Sundays he was in Russia. The churches were filled to bursting, but with old people exclusively, he noted.

He also went to synagogues, talked to priests and academicians, visited trials and talked afterwards to the judge about his salary. Miller remembers going to a library with Trudeau once and asking for works by Dostoyevsky, who was in official disrepute. They couldn't be found on the shelves.

The other delegates spent little time with Trudeau but remember him clearly.

"Trudeau didn't contribute very much. He attended some sessions but he didn't make any serious impact," said Cowan. "He didn't go over there because he was pro-Soviet, he went over there as a lark.

"He loved to go to the Bolshoi ballet. He had a trick there which I saw him do several times. He wouldn't applaud, he would stand in the aisle and just fall flat on his hands without bending his knees. Then he'd race backstage afterwards to try to pick up a ballerina or something."

Miller remembers Trudeau being so tremendously impressed with the ballerina, Lepechinskaia, that when he returned to Canada he took up ballet for a time.

Freeman also recalls Trudeau from the Bolshoi, because he would stand up on his seat and cheer. To him, Trudeau was a "footloose, happy-go-lucky, young fellow" who would make a "beeline for the big buffets they served with lavish foods and stuff himself with caviar".

At one point, Trudeau says he almost got himself in trouble with his Soviet hosts.

"Impressed with seeing in public and private places in town and in the country, busts, statues, photos, paintings . . . representing the Father of the People, the Idol of the Working Masses . . . the Great Comrade Stalin, I affectionately threw a snowball at a statue of him where he looked particularly kind.

"Scandal! But my hosts expressed more pain than anger. And so I was able to continue speaking about Tito, to ask for works by Trotski in libraries and generally to talk about a hangman's rope on death row."

Trudeau admitted that the Canadian delegation was made of "lightweights" and said he could describe them that way "without injuring the vanity of my likeable, fellow, English Canadian citizens". But aside from the Bolshoi or a chance meeting during the conference itself, Trudeau didn't see the Toronto members of the delegation very much.

At one point, the conference was addressed by Vasil V. Kuznetsov, who was described as a Soviet trade union leader—but who was later exposed as a major-general in the KGB.[6]

Miller recalls that Trudeau spent much of his time with three members of the large British delegation: Alexander Cairncross; the late Professor Maurice Herbert Dobb and Professor Joan Vidlet Robinson. Trudeau himself remembers Joan Robinson, whom he described as "distinguished and non-communist," as a member of the International Initiating Committee based in Denmark from which he had received his invitation to the conference.

The three whom Trudeau met were poles apart in their views. Cairncross, now Sir Alexander, was a distinguished, moderate economist at Glasgow University, while the other two were from Cambridge University.

Dobb had been an economics tutor at Trinity College there when he formed the first communist cell, into which he recruited Harold "Kim" Philby, who was later exposed as an infamous Soviet agent.

"Without Dobb," says one account of him,[7] "Trinity could not have become in the early thirties the undisputed centre of Cambridge communism . . . Among many economists whose views he helped form was his contemporary, Joan Robinson, then an assistant lecturer."

Trudeau, these three, Peter Wiles of Oxford University, P. Sraffa of Cambridge University, Professor Madge of Birmingham University and Miller got into extensive conversations with Soviet economists, including two, two-hour meetings at the Academy of Science. Wiles later summed up their interviews and published the gist of them in an article in Soviet Studies, an academic review.

Robinson, while she can remember everyone else in the meetings, can't remember Trudeau at all. She remembered Wiles, though.

"Wiles was very anti-Soviet. He was rather a sort of rogue elephant at the meeting."

He, in turn, didn't have much use for Robinson or Dobb. "I refused to be taken in by bullshit—and they're a bunch of bullshitters."

The conference wound up Saturday, April 12, and the Canadian delegates headed home with the exception of Miller and Trudeau. Miller had been invited to "help fill the stands with foreigners" during a celebration in Peking by Nan Han-cheng, the president of the People's Bank of China.

He accepted and urged Trudeau to go with him, but Nan wouldn't invite Trudeau because, said Miller, he looked too unconventional with his cravat and sandals.

Trudeau decided to stay another two weeks in the Soviet Union. First he headed west to Minsk in White Russia and then south through the Ukraine, where the people had been starved and slaughtered into submission under Stalin's collectivization plan two decades previously. He visited Kharkov and then continued south to Rostov, on the Don River, across the Sea of Azov from the Crimea. He followed the Black Sea Coast southeast, seeing the Caucasus Mountains and the Georgian countryside, to Tbilisi, near the Turkish border.

His wanderings came to an abrupt end when he said the Soviets "coldly demanded that I leave the U.S.S.R."

Trudeau headed back to Canada to write about his trip for Le Devoir, but several accounts had already preceded his.

The propaganda organ of the Communist Party of Canada, the Canadian Tribune, had already carried the impressions of three delegation members, Hancock, Freeman and Cowan.

The Tribune had been dividing its headlines for months between allegations of U.S. germ warfare by Communist Chinese and Dr. James Endicott (then chairman of the Canadian Peace Congress), and the Moscow economic conference.

In an interview with the Tribune, Freeman said that "tremendous progress was evident everywhere in Moscow, the stores filled to overflowing, fully laden shelves, rapid construction going on and a spirit of confidence in the future".

Hancock warned that Canada was "missing the boat" in international trade. "Unless Canadian exporters speed up and make at least the initial contacts, every other country in the world will beat us out to these great opportunities."

Cowan, in a joint press release with Freeman, said he was perturbed "to travel through Europe and discover how isolated Canada is becoming economically".

Trudeau wrote a seven-part series for Le Devoir starting Saturday, June 14, which was heralded by a front page banner urging readers to follow his articles. The articles, each headed by the byline, "Pierre Elliott-Trudeau," not only dealt with the conference itself, but with his reasons for going and the U.S.S.R. in general.

He opened with the observation that "for many people, the Soviet Union is hell, and you don't put a foot in it without making a pact with the devil. This prejudice prevented many economists and businessmen from attending the International Economic Conference at Moscow.

"What would you have to agree to, to have the right to go to Moscow to converse with the most eminent economists, applaud Lepechinskaia and Ulanova at the Bolshoi and gulp spoonfuls of caviar?"

Trudeau listed the conditions laid down by the International Initiating Committee and said they sounded acceptable, so he accepted.

About 500 others from 49 countries, of all political persuasions, also accepted, he noted. "And all these people weren't supporters of Satan, it's useful to underline. For certain governments and newspapers have tried to make us believe that and their opinions have become dogma in all the political and financial circles where they have a lot of influence."

He didn't think his fellow Quebecers would condemn him, for "as anti-Bolshevik as they are, they have a healthy distrust for their neighbours 'over the border' . . . "

All the same, Trudeau said he had qualms about going to the conference. The communists had unleashed their peace campaign to sow disunity in western peoples, he said, and the Moscow conference could be another such tactic.

The difference between the two was that while he could see through the peace campaign right away, he wasn't sure about the conference. "If through fear, or necessity, or reason, the Politbureau's men really want to develop multi-lateral trade, should we refuse to hear their propositions?"

If it was just another ruse, the West could always continue the blockade. Those considerations aside, he said, the conference would give a few hundred westerners the chance to meet their Iron Curtain counterparts which "would serve to lay a more human foundation for future meetings".

So Trudeau said on that basis he decided to go and soon discovered the Russian people to be "kind but sickeningly conventional". He had decided to act in Moscow as he would have elsewhere, but he soon found brakes were put on any independent behaviour.

"Thus, if I used Stalin as a target quite naturally, it was only because I had also thrown snowballs at Wilfrid Laurier on Parliament Hill. And I refused to follow my guide in the Kremlin for the same reasons as my guide in the Vatican caves."

He found the beliefs of Russians close to those of St. Thomas Aquinas. "Stalinism has often been compared to a religion, but you really have to go to the U.S.S.R. to feel how blind their faith is . . . Marx the prophet; Lenin the forerunner; and Stalin made man.

"The people seemed happy with their relative prosperity," he thought, but added that "when the alternative to believing is dying, it's not surprising to find that the majority are believers."

There was another side to their national character. "They are determined to be strong whatever price they have to pay. That's why western politicians make me laugh when they depict Russians as a people who only live in the hope of being free of the Stalinist yoke. They won't commit this spiritual sin. On the contrary, the more they feel their country is menaced from the outside, the more they will rally around their leaders, hardening themselves into rock-like resolve.

"They proved that soon after the revolution when they heroically repulsed western and Polish interventionists. They proved it again against the Nazis, to the great relief of the civilized world.[8]

"On the other hand, a long peaceful period would make defences against 'counter-revolutionaries' useless for Stalinist authorities and maybe they would think about dropping them a little ... "

Trudeau reviewed the average income and cost of living for a worker and concluded that "everyone is clothed modestly and often eats sparingly. But no one looks hungry.

"What's certain is that the standard of living is steadily rising, and this is working strongly for the regime. Moscow almost has the air of a prosperous city ... and this isn't only true for Moscow. I passed through other large cities and ... found signs of development everywhere."

True, he saw queues almost everywhere as well, "but you've got to recognize that at least Soviet economists have resolved the problem of inflation without producing unemployment.

"Without doubt, the country is progressing tremendously. But it's progressing exactly in the way the planners want it, not the way the citizens want it."

Compared to citizens of capitalist countries, Soviet citizens lived pretty poorly, Trudeau wrote. But the Russian "consoles himself with the thought that the whole Soviet economy is geared to the common good, and not to the good of one class.

"That's what's called economic democracy in popular democracies."

As far as the actual economic conference went, Trudeau admitted readily that the communists launched and organized it, but didn't see that as a bad thing in itself. As long as it was kept open and politically neutral, he believed it was a good forum for letting potential enemies get together and talk.

During the conference, he realized that the Soviets hadn't taken the least risk of losing control, and had the governing committees stacked in their favour, but they didn't abuse that control.

During the conference he said several trade deals were concluded, such as a British offer to sell cotton to the Communist Chinese.[9]

"Obviously it was a small beginning. But don't expect anything bigger when the conference was boycotted by the country which so completely dominates trade in the non-communist world.

"The important thing was to take the first steps, and show that all capital and markets weren't controlled by the United States."

It was also important to show that India and Latin America understood that "the ubiquity of the dollar doesn't happen without a threat to national sovereignty". But Trudeau didn't think the ruble should replace the dollar. What he wanted to see was diversification and interdependence in world trade.

In the last of his seven articles, which was entitled "They Had Three Revolutions For This?", Trudeau looked at the Soviet Union as a whole.

While he observed that "unhappily, the revolution hadn't destroyed the old Russian mania for uniforms" and that the Kremlin nourished a hate among the people for foreign governments, he saw no evidence that the Soviets had their eyes fixed on territorial expansion as Hitler and Mussolini had.

"On the contrary, one of the principal concerns of the state seems to be to better the material welfare of its citizens. And if they are happy with a system which raises their standard of living slowly but surely, the present government doesn't have any worries for a long time . . .

"Those who can remember the Tzarist era see that there has been a general improvement. (It's useless to ask them at what price. Even by 1925, Beraud remarked that they didn't remember the blood.) Others, less than 40 years old . . . have an intransigence, a puritanism, an admirable faith in their (red) star that characterize true believers.

"It reminds me a bit of a young Englishman during the best days of the Empire. Or better still, Americans during Lincoln's time, hardily pushing to the last frontiers, building up their power and riches—all transfigured by the vision of a world pregnant with change."

Later he said he thought a lot of the Soviet leaders' hate for the U.S. was simple envy.

"This damn capitalist country has attained a high degree of material prosperity with ridiculous ease, but the U.S.S.R., despite all its efforts, is still a thousand leagues away from its heaven on earth.

"In my efforts to understand the U.S.S.R., I've always tried to explain the rigours of the regime away with the necessity of protecting the revolution from enemies without and within.

"But I can't really see where the revolution is found anymore.

"Look at liberal Canada, comrades, socialist Sweden, and labour-socialist Australia, where capitalism is little by little being discredited by organized workers insisting on justice.

"They sincerely believe they can obtain that while respecting the meaning of Christianity, through democratic means and within the constitution: they don't put the same emphasis as you do on the gospel according to St. Marx, but is that any reason why you should detest the good that they do?

"I still believe that from the material point of view (and I don't say anything about spiritual needs) your system can be excellent for countries such as yours . . . and I add that in your country I never saw opulence displayed which was an insult to a great many people like I have often seen in countries on the other side of the Iron Curtain.

"But despite everything, open the borders of the U.S.S.R. a little, and the comrades will be able to establish for themselves that what is revolutionary over there is reactionary for most western countries."

Trudeau concluded his article and his series with an appeal to the Soviets.

"If you're really working for the happiness of the people, and not Russian influence, it seems to me that you've got to be a little more Trotskyite, a little more Titoist.

"In every country, always be justice's agent of ferment, bring the Left together, and rise up against exploitation of man by man. But wouldn't you have to stop referring everywhere to Mister Stalin and to the glorious example of the U.S.S.R.? Only then would all the forces of the Left be able to rally together and strengthen themselves with bonds of friendship between all progressive countries.

"You would thus form a true Popular Front against reactionary forces that would know no boundaries."

About two months before this final article, on April 23, 1952, another article appeared on the front page of Le Devoir, headed "The Names of the Canadians Who went to Moscow Are Revealed". The story listed the six men and Mrs. Freeman, whose names had been read out at a meeting of the parliamentary external affairs committee the day before by Herbert Moran, the assistant under-secretary of state for external affairs. Le Devoir didn't mention, however, that when Moran had described the six as "businessmen", committee chairman J. A. Bradette said Teeple had been a communist candidate against him in the past elections and "I know what kind of business he runs".

Moran said the six had attended the conference at their own expense with no support from the Canadian government.

In the autumn of 1952, Trudeau gave a talk to the International Relations Club of the University of Montreal on the conference. He told students much of what he said in his Le Devoir series and added that the conference had demonstrated that even if opposing governments wouldn't discuss issues together for fear of losing face, individuals from those countries could at least gather to discuss trade.

"It's obvious that Russians are citizens of a dictatorial, monolithic state ... the U.S.S.R. isn't the paradise they want us to believe—there's no real equality ... there has been a bourgeois revolution, that's to say, they've gone from the feudal system to the bourgeois system with its (state) capitalism, its inequalities and its evolution, which is far from being revolutionary. In fact, the worker has a lot more importance and influence in our democratic country than in the U.S.S.R."

Trudeau's series had not gone unnoticed in Montreal's religious community. The Reverend J. B. Desrosiers, editor of the religious review "Nos Cours" read it and found it "one-sided". His opinion carried some weight, as Nos Cours was the organ of the Pope Pius XI Institute, attached to the faculty of theology at the University of Montreal, and was published under the sanction of Paul-Émile Cardinal Leger of Montreal.

Desrosiers decided a formal reply to Trudeau was warranted and the Reverend Léopold Braun was chosen for the task. Braun was fluent in Russian, Polish, German and several other languages and had spent from 1934 to 1945 living in Moscow. He had left for a European trip shortly before Trudeau's articles appeared, and it was only on November 15, 1952, that his lengthy reply appeared in Nos Cours.

He said Trudeau's series was "strongly one-sided" and full of errors and faulty conclusions. Braun wanted to believe that Trudeau hadn't deliberately led his readers astray, but had to say that Trudeau's observations would be more at home in a book of fairy tales than in a newspaper report.

Trudeau had said "for many people, the Soviet Union is hell". "There's more truth in that assertion than the author seems to believe. Of 200 million Russians in this hermetically sealed country, 16 to 20 million of them are vegetating and rotting in concentration camps," wrote Braun. "These weren't shown to the economists at the conference."

The Soviet state didn't stand up very well when compared either with the Tzarist regime or the Nazis. "In 35 years of the Marxist regime, of Bolshevik atheism, the number of dead, interned or deported Russians reached the frightful total of about 25 million! Lenin's successors... have exceeded the record of atrocities committed by the Nazis. At the height of Imperial power, a total of 298,577 were detained, against the communist total of 16 million.

"And with all that, our author dares to speak of what he calls the 'unanimous support' of the people for the regime?

"It makes Mr. Trudeau laugh when he hears western politicians say—with reason—that Russians live in the hope of being free of the Stalinist yoke. But that's exactly what Russians hope for with all their souls . . . You could see it in the camps for displaced persons who had left the Soviet hell . . . you could see it in the millions of civilians and soldiers of the Red Army who gave themselves up to the Germans in the first hours of the invasion . . . you could see it in the innumerable displaced persons who committed suicide, many of whom were to be forcefully repatriated thanks to the Potsdam Agreement. If Mr. Trudeau still wants to laugh after hearing these facts, so clearly ignored by him, he should know that his laugh will echo that of Vishinsky, Stalin, Beria and company.

"Why doesn't Mr. Trudeau tell the readers of Le Devoir that light and heavy industrial production has been channelled almost totally to preparations for war?

"Mr Trudeau . . . said the prices of certain commodities were officially lowered . . . [he] rendered a great service to the yappings of communist boasting. But in Moscow, what happened when the lower prices were announced? Naturally everyone raced to the stores . . . but there was nothing to sell."

One week after it appeared in Nos Cours, Braun's article was reprinted as a seven-part series in two French Canadian dailies, Le Droit and Action Catholique, in Ottawa and Quebec City. "The Hard Realities of the Red Paradise," read the first headline in Le Droit, on November 22.

Then, to make matters worse, a Jesuit Priest, Joseph Ledit, wrote a two-part feature for Le Droit on December 1, entitled "A Popular Front in Quebec?"

He traced a number of popular fronts engineered in Quebec by communists since the thirties until "the pilgrimages to Moscow started. First it was Mr. Trudeau, whose articles appeared in Le Devoir, and who was answered by Father Braun . . . After Mr. Trudeau it was Mr. Filion [Gerard Filion, editor-in-chief of Le Devoir]."

Trudeau decided to reply to his critics and an article by him appeared in Le Droit, December 18, entitled "The Response of Mr. Pierre Elliott Trudeau to the Criticisms of Father Braun".

"I'm opposed to communism, but that didn't stop me from going to the U.S.S.R. for thirty days for the International Economic Conference in April.

"The reverend bases his articles on his experience from the beginning of March, 1934 to December 27, 1945, which makes him singularly unqualified to discuss my observations, on prices and salaries for example, made in April 1952."

He scolded Braun for not being up on his theory and suggested he read "The State and The Revolution" by Lenin and quoted writings by Stalin to him.

"It appears then that on the face of it, Father Braun was not qualified in theory or fact to make any 'detailed commentary' on my articles."

Even when he criticized the Soviet system, Braun had him seem like a crypto-communist by nuances. A lot had been made of his statement that the people seemed to give unanimous support to the regime. But Trudeau noted that Braun had not quoted his next statement: "When the alternative to believing (in Stalin) is dying, it's not surpising to find that the majority are believers."

Trudeau concluded his reply to Braun with "assuredly, each is free to practise anti-communism whatever way he wants to; and clearly my style is not the same as Father Braun's. But does the reverend want me to think that he's not so much a danger to the communists, as he is a nuisance to me?"

While it was a light-hearted, public taunt, indications are that privately Trudeau was incensed with Braun's attack.

Marcel Rioux, a contributor to Cité Libre and an old Paris hand, recalls staying at Trudeau's house on McCulloch Street before Christmas.

"We were having some milk and cookies one night before going to bed and he asked me if I had read his arguments with Father Braun. I said no, and he said 'You must read it. Read it and tell me if I am right or wrong'."

Rioux recalls he was very intense and practically ordered him to read his article.

There was a short breather in the Braun-Trudeau battle for Christmas, but it resumed January 10, in Nos Cours again.

Trudeau's Le Droit article was reprinted, followed by another by Father Braun and a piece by the editor, Desrosiers.

Braun said it was "far from being proven" that Trudeau was really opposed to communism and said he had been used for Soviet propaganda like several others Braun had known. More than that, by Trudeau's claim that freedom of religion was very much alive in Russia he had "done a great service to Soviet propaganda".

Not only had Le Devoir, with his articles, appeared in Montreal and other cities, but Trudeau himself gave several speeches in cities around the province.

"While it's true that Mr. Trudeau mentioned inequalities, planned famines, counter-revolutions and the suppression of millions of 'Kulaks,' the balance of his series leans all too noticeably toward admiration and apology for a system which is choking the people ... "

Nos Cours hadn't quite finished with Trudeau. The review's editor wrote: "As far as we're concerned, he's opposed to communism. In fact, in his articles there are a fair number of criticisms of communism ... what needs to be noted in these articles are all the half-truths and serious insinuations, and at the very least that certain conclusions serve communist propaganda."

As that edition of Nos Cours appeared, the nationalist magazine, L'Action Nationale, edited by André Laurendeau (Trudeau's associate from the League for the Defence of Canada era), was just going to press.

Both Laurendeau and Francois-Albert Angers wrote defences of Trudeau in what was to be the final chapter in the war of words over Trudeau's Moscow visit and subsequent series.

"Has a witchhunt begun?" asked Laurendeau. The "sudden unleashing of hostilities and irrational criticism" by Braun constituted a fundamental change in atmosphere.

"It's already been written that even if a witchhunt is raging in the United States, at least it hasn't crossed our borders. That was true at the time. But is it still? I wonder if we're not witnessing right now our first 'witchhunts'."

Angers agreed saying he didn't think Trudeau's "objective, well-measured and clear" conclusions could lead one to believe he was a philosophical or crypto-communist. He then commenced a 23-page defence of Trudeau, citing his criticisms of the Soviet system and in turn criticizing Braun.

Angers was convinced he had to come to Trudeau's defence because Braun's articles were "the proof of the presence of a spirit dangerous to the very cause we all want to serve: the cause of Christianity's future in a world which communism is splitting asunder and infiltrating everywhere, to the point where Christians are beginning to look at themselves and distrust each other."[10]

FOOTNOTES CHAPTER 5

1. From a white paper released by the U.S. state department in September, 1952.
2. Financial Post, March 8, 1952.
3. From a U.S. state department bulletin, March 14, 1952.
4. Gazette, Montreal, March 11, 1952.
5. Most of these details on Trudeau's trip to Russia are taken from a series of articles he wrote in Le Devoir from June 14 to June 21, 1952.
6. John Barron, "KGB," Readers' Digest Association, New York, 1974.
7. Patrick Seale and Maureen McConville, "Philby, the Long Road to Moscow," Hamish Hamilton Ltd., London, 1973.
8. Trudeau could not have heard of the Russian General Vlassov, a senior cog in the Russian war machine in the Second World War. He was anti-semitic and anti-Stalinist, and after being captured by the Germans during their offensive, joined their side and fought at Stalingrad at the head of a Russian army. In fact, by the beginning of 1944, it is estimated that 650,000 Russians were fighting Stalin.
9. This agreement, which might have been concluded in London before the conference if the Chinese hadn't wanted strategic materials as well, later fell through for this very reason.
10. L'Action Nationale, January, 1953.

6

Drifting

When Trudeau returned to Canada after his European and Russian travels he discovered he had been left out of an ambitious project by his friends at Cité Libre.

In the four years between 1948 and 1952 there had been extensive contacts between Esprit and Cité Libre. Albert Béguin and Henri-Irenée Marrou, the publisher of Esprit and the review's frequent contributor, had visited Montreal for meetings with the Cité Libre group. So had Jean-Marie Domenach, the editor-in-chief, who recalled staying at Trudeau's home in Outremont.

In early 1952 the liaison culminated in a proposal by Béguin that the Cité Libre group produce an entire issue of Esprit devoted to developments in French Canada. They gladly took up the offer and Maurice Blain, Jean-Marc Léger, Gerard Pelletier, Reginald Boisvert and Jean-Guy Blain each wrote an article.

In addition, both Frank Scott, a professor of law at McGill University in Montreal, and Jean-Charles Falardeau, of the faculty of social sciences of Laval University in Quebec City, contributed. Scott had come to know the Cité Libristes through his contacts in the socialist movement in Quebec, his involvement in the strike at Asbestos and French Canadian literary circles. He was also the director of Recherches Sociales, a social action and analysis group funded by a wealthy socialist. Others involved in that group were Léger, André Laurendeau, Gerard

68

Filion, Jacques Perrault (owner of Le Devoir), Trudeau and Pelletier.

The special Esprit issue was doubly important. Not only did it enhance the prestige of Cité Libristes among the left-wing elite in Quebec, but in Domenach's words, "with our issue they were 'discovered'" in France.

In writing the foreword to the edition, Marrou noted that although it had been produced by Canadians, it was nevertheless a true issue of Esprit. The Cité Libristes weren't foreign contributors, but "friends, companions".

When he had first visited Montreal in 1948, he had been surprised to see how much influence Esprit and its philosophy had on the intellectual elite. For the youth there, Esprit formed a rallying point, a catalyst.

"The group which has produced this edition, and which expresses itself so courageously through the review Cité Libre, is a genuine Canadian team of Esprit.

"It's a team few in number, but of high quality; these are my friends . . . I'll simply say that these young men aren't 'intellectuals' in the bad sense of the word . . . most of them are involved with the rank and file working class and work, as journalists or lawyers, in the service of powerful labour organizations on which the future of Canada seems to hinge."

Pelletier's contribution was entitled "On a Spiritual Proletariat" and traced the effect rapid industrialization had on the church's relation with a new urban proletariat. In 1890, 37 per cent of Quebec's population was urban, but 60 years later only 30 per cent of the population was rural.

When peasants arrived in a large city, there was scarcely any tradition to replace their old one except that of the bourgeoisie.

One could see in urban parishes a slow but steady reduction in the number of faithful, because the church hadn't adapted itself to urban realities. If the church didn't adapt itself soon, he predicted, the trickle would become a flood.

But there were signs of change within the clergy, which might allow it to retain the following of the working masses. All the same, the change hung in the balance, a delicate balance.

"We're walking a tightrope. The least puff of wind might

mean death for us. Anti-communism, for example, when it assumes the face of hysteria in North America, threatens our evolution. For anti-Russian panic tends to throw us back onto our traditional positions of defensiveness and negative attitudes; it forces a siege mentality on us, which is hardly favourable for an attempt at self-criticism."

Jean-Charles Falardeau described the prevalence and power of the church in French Canadian society, and Maurice Blain discussed and criticized the oppression of the clergy.

Léger looked at the Canadian political system and observed that the Liberal and Conservative parties consisted above all of powerful election machines, and were interested almost exclusively in the gaining, exercising and conserving of power.

The CCF was described as the only national Canadian party based on an ideology. But the fact that it was identified as being basically an "English" party and "dangerously socialist" by many conservative Quebecers had always prevented it from gaining any real power in the province.

Of the two other parties, the Liberals had held power almost continuously since the first war, when the Conservatives had endorsed overseas conscription. The Liberal Party had tactical superiority over their rivals, as they were less rigid in their policies—in fact they could be described as unscrupulous and Machiavellian.

The church in Quebec could hardly be expected to sit back and be criticized as oppressive. A Jesuit priest, Father Richard Arès, responded to the charges in the Jesuits' influential review, Relations.

His response was reasoned and low-key. "It's heard everywhere that French Canada is now passing through a grave crisis ... for a small group of young intellectuals, the crisis, above all, is a religious one, and is shown in the growing tension between the laity and the clergy ...

"But first, is it really true that there is a crisis? I'll start by noting that a certain amount of anti-clericalism in French Canada isn't a new phenomenon." Two recent examples were the special issue of Esprit on French Canada and the existence of Cité Libre.

Cité Libre was the mouthpiece of a group of young intellectuals who said they were "dissatisfied", but whom others called "malcontents and rebellious". If they were anti-clerical, they said it was in the name of liberty and religion.

This group perhaps wouldn't have drawn any attention if they hadn't set out their ideas and demands in Esprit in a manner some found scandalous and shocking. Le Devoir had helped publicize the edition with a story on it filed by their Paris correspondent.

The young intellectuals were rebelling against "accepted systems, established order, conformity, traditionalism and conservatism". This was nothing very new for youth anywhere in the world, and might be put down as youthful exuberance.[1]

The young intellectuals of Cité Libre had a chance to rebel and wax indignant over the provincial elections of July, 1952— once more Maurice Duplessis was swept to power at the head of his National Union party.

Trudeau was plainly disgusted at the results. He subsequently lent his pages not only to a spokesman for the socialist party, but also to Pierre Gélinas, the director of agitation and propaganda for the communist party in Quebec. Those two, with three others from established parties who had contested the election, wrote their interpretations of the election's outcome.

Then Trudeau subjected Duplessis, his party, and French Canada's morality to a lengthy analysis.

"Our profound immorality has got to be explained. In our relations with the State, we're fairly immoral: we corrupt civil servants, we bribe our members of parliament, we put pressure on the courts...

"To say that 'Latin people don't take very well to democracy' and that 'Nordic people have a sharper sense of civic duty' explains nothing at all: we must find out why that is."

After the British conquered French Canada, French Canadians made up their minds to "abuse, not use," the parliamentary system. They played the parliamentary game, but they didn't believe the basic principles upon which it was founded. They were so worried about preserving their national identity that they subordinated the national good to French Canada's good, and lost their sense of political morality in the process.

"Our sense of civic duty was perverted; we became opportun-

71

ists . . . it must be recognized that Catholics—and I say it much to our great shame—as a whole have rarely been supporters of democracy."

French Canada's answer to the Great Depression was to demand that the State re-affirm its nationalism. "As far as we were concerned, our misfortunes weren't the result of the economic system, but of a system dominated by 'The English'."

Since 1948, however, the government had become more interventionist economically, and the question had to be asked: "For whose advantage should the state intervene, for an ethnic group, or a social class?

"Ideological questions have acquired an importance they never had before in our province, and it's become urgent that we elect candidates capable of defending these ideologies."

Instead, an inept government had practically bought its way into office, and "as long as it takes that much money to elect a government in Quebec, the population will be sure to have policies dictated solely by high finance: which is to say, the State will continue to be a tool of economic dictatorship."

Canadians often scorned the "political immaturity" of Americans, but in one respect they were a long way behind them. Governor Stevenson, in the last American elections, had proposed this principle: "Every candidate for high political office should disclose his personal financial condition."

Who could drag the province out of its profound immorality? Certainly not high finance, which had a vested interest in preserving the status quo.

It might come from the working class—maybe helped by some quasi-proletarian white collar workers.

Since the Asbestos strike in 1949, the workers had learned that "their struggle was not against the English, Protestants or Jews, but against financiers, or better, against a certain conception of capitalism".

They also learned two political principles: the government can exert a lot of economic influence on certain sectors of the population, and when a government is caught in a conflict of interest, it should act on behalf of the sector which brought it to power.

Trudeau then looked at the election results themselves. The

National Union had won basically a rural victory, capturing a total of 68 seats of 92, with half the popular vote. The Liberal Party, on the other hand, had only taken 23 seats with 45 per cent of the popular vote. The way the electoral map was drawn, if Duplessis' party could hold the support of the rural vote through appeals to nationalism, it would probably win the next election as well.

The Liberals had increased their popular vote by nine per cent because their platform had contained social reform measures which appealed to workers. But on the other hand, their "radically-tainted liberalism" had scared off those who "get frightened at the word 'left': federal bigwigs, for example, and the business community, who had temporarily cut off their backing."

The party had developed a split personality—grouping those Liberals who merely wanted to protect their interests and those "who called themselves Liberals for ideological motives". The former group had installed Georges-Henri Lapalme as leader of the party because it thought it could control him, but he had "escaped enough of this control to give courage to the second group".

Jean-Louis Gagnon was obviously in the second group, which was why he underlined the importance of a social ideology and a movement based on militants... But the powers of the party "probably wouldn't allow them to establish positions sufficiently socially-oriented to rally the main progressive forces of the province..." That would probably result in the Liberals losing the next election.

Unless the Liberals listened to the warning, "you must move to the left", and became an embryonic social movement, they would disappear, crushed between the conservative National Union and a left-wing party which would form without it.

The socialist CCF party had, as usual, done terribly in the elections. It was still perceived as fundamentally an "English" party despite the courageous efforts of Mme. Thérèse Casgrain, the leader of the CCF in Quebec, to change this perception. "Only slowly can she uproot ancient prejudices, while waiting for the blooming of a social conscience in Quebec."

But while the religious and ethnic reflexes of Quebec's working class prevented them from accepting the CCF, on the other hand, "the clear-sighted instincts which have for so long guided the working class in the choice of its means of action must not be underestimated.

"It seems to me that those of the labour movement who supported Liberal candidates in the last elections committed an error. Old parties willingly accept new blood—but it never changes them into socially-oriented parties... the labour unions should have used the last elections to campaign for intensive education...

"But if the working class fails in its mission to cleanse Quebec society; and if, as a consequence, it fails to express its ideological force through democratic means... then it could suffer a profound crisis, for the oppressed masses might accept the help of the only party to promise them the dictatorship of the proletariat, whose efficacy doesn't necessarily wait for constitutional means."

That party was the Labour Progressive Party [the Communist Party of Canada changed its name in 1942], which he described as "without age, without country and numerically insignificant". Gelinas had proposed a common front to fight Duplessis, but Trudeau didn't foresee it happening unless the working class was thwarted democratically.

"That's why I find so clumsy those people who try to fight communism by fomenting fear and a hysterical hate of it. Employing these techniques weakens one's democratic sense... In Quebec it's the height of irrationality because our people have all sorts of excellent reasons for rejecting communism, spiritual, political and economic...

"In my opinion, structural reforms will only succeed with the support of new social forces...

"I conclude that until the new order, social forces must be allowed to express themselves calmly and rationally... Experience has taught us, through certain strikes, that oppression engenders violence; and it's precisely to avoid that, in any form, that we should rectify our profound immorality."[2]

Cité Libre had clearly made its mark by the end of 1952. Early in the new year Time magazine ran a story on it under the heading "Duel with Orthodoxy".

Time described Cité Libre as a "French-language publication of, by and for intellectuals who have no love for ivory towers". It traced Cité Libre's foundations, reviewed the special December issue on Quebec's election and quoted Trudeau and Pelletier.

"The nine men who publish Cité Libre are not in it for the money; profit on one issue seldom is more than a piddling $25. They find their reward in politely criticizing Quebec institutions and practices they feel need correction or reformation. All are Roman Catholics. But they have not hesitated to question the clergy's powerful sway over provincial life.

"'We have a tendency to go against the current,' Pelletier told Time."

But the prestige and recognition afforded by the Time article was more than offset by another in a Montreal French weekly, La Patrie. It featured an interview with Patrick Walsh, a Royal Canadian Mounted Police informant who had "come in from the cold". Walsh had infiltrated high levels of the Communist Party of Canada and travelled widely on its behalf.

Walsh told La Patrie of the danger of communist infiltration in Quebec's intelligentsia. He named one communist-financed magazine, Place Publique, and said that while many intellectuals associated with it weren't communists, they collaborated with it because of a "literary trend".

"They [communists] have tried to set up a cell in another intellectual group called Cité Libre; the director of agitation and propaganda [Gelinas] contributed to it. This strange collaboration between communists and Catholics isn't anything new; in France two Catholic magazines collaborate with the communists."

The charge that communists were trying to set up a cell in Cité Libre had to be answered by the group. Charles Lussier did so two months later in a two-page article entitled "Mr. Pat Walsh, Communists and Cité Libre".

"Pat Walsh, under the pretext of an interview, revealed the existence of collaboration between the communist party and a group called 'Cité Libre'." Normally the magazine wouldn't have bothered answering the charge, but because of the "collective hysteria for communists" it had decided to do so.

"Those who have read and understood us know that all members of the team called 'Cité Libre' are militants in circles which are fundamentally Christian and anti-communist."

In preparing Cité Libre's special election issue, it had been decided that it would only be fair if all provincial parties in the election were asked their views. A National Union supporter had contributed an article, and Cité Libre could hardly be accused of collaborating with them![3]

Pelletier and Trudeau teamed up in the same issue to write a long, two-part article, "Material for an Inquiry into Clericalism".

Trudeau must have smiled when he prefaced his article with a quote from Father Léopold Braun, who had attacked his series on Moscow in Nos Cours: "It's up to us to open the frontiers of our hearts.

"Let it be understood at the very beginning that I'm anti-clericalist," wrote Trudeau. "(I write that with no shame, and with the firm conviction that many will read that I'm anti-clerical.)"

He opposed the Church's influence in temporal and political affairs but admitted that the Church's role "wasn't easy, particularly in a society in transition like ours.

"I never would have had the presumption to broach the problem myself, of the relation of the clergy to the temporal world, if I hadn't been the victim of an odious attack. But two priests are guilty of libelling me.

"If a priest wants to get involved in temporal affairs, he should do it as a common citizen, and not with the prestige that his habit lends him . . .

"If these reflections are just, I have the right to say that the priests who profited from their priestly privileges to slanderously attack my political opinions and more, to defame my honour, are guilty of uncalled-for abuse."

Braun had used his series in Le Devoir as a pretext to "shower me with all the disgraces that his morbid hatred had really destined for the men of the Kremlin." He also criticized Father Desrosiers, the editor of Nos Cours, for agreeing to print his response to Braun in Nos Cours only after a month and a half of repeated requests, and then only in a shortened form and followed by another article by Braun.

"I don't propose to reply to the venomous, dishonest response of Father Braun . . . and Father Braun didn't respond to my initial defence, but simply repeated his initial vituperation, with more lies and insults.

"In appearance, there was the whole arsenal of the church hierarchy mobilized against me . . .

"In a way (and while the Pope prays for Stalin and intercedes for the Rosenbergs), the Keepers of the Light in Quebec are gathering denunciations and defamations, in the name of Catholicism (theirs, evidently), but to the great advantage of the National Union party, international capitalism and all the interests written in history's margin. They want to make Quebec the last bastion of clericalism and of political reaction . . . what a colonial mentality, what servile spirits!

"Until now, it was to Canada's honour that this variety of witchhunt was rarely practised here. But it must however be regretted that Nos Cours, under the sanction of Cardinal Leger, and L'Action Catholique, the newspaper of Monseigneur Roy [Louis-Phillippe, the archbishop of Quebec City], took the initiative in importing across the border a tactic of Senator McCarthy's to make a 'critical examination' of my articles.

"Be on your guard that hatred and persecution don't come into Canada through the doors of the Church."

It was just as well that the Pope was praying for the soul of Stalin, who had died March 5—there were few in Russia who would. His name would be long remembered, and not just as the man who had led Russia to victory over Hitler in the Second World War.

In the decade after that war the world had been in turmoil, with governments being bloodily overthrown and new political movements mushrooming everywhere. Trudeau didn't see Canada's place in this world as segregated or disconnected, so when his country's elections were called for August 10, 1953, he saw them in an international context.

"The advent of total war contributed—more than is generally thought—to the promotion of popular masses. . . . In a way, the idea of democracy made gigantic progress everywhere in the world between 1939 and 1945. In Europe, in Asia, oligarchic or dictatorial powers fell before popular governments. And elsewhere, where democracy was already well-known, it would henceforth be otherwise comprised.

"Whole peoples were sliding to the left. One talked about the 'welfare state.'... three Commonwealth countries gave themselves labour-socialist governments. Socialism consolidated its position in Scandinavia and progressed in the main western European countries.... The Republicans were easily defeated in the United States in 1944 and 1948."

Events unfolded similarly in Canada: in 1945, "a left-wing wind blew over the country". The socialist CCF took power in Saskatchewan, and became the official opposition in Manitoba, Nova Scotia, British Columbia and Ontario. In the federal elections, the socialists took 31 seats, up from eight in 1940, and communists won 100,000 votes.

"But post-war reaction was plotted in Canada as elsewhere. The 'elite' invited the people to reflect on the prosperity brought about by 'free enterprise', on the recession of 1948 caused by unreasonable demands by the people, on Marxism and its international repercussions.

"The desired sickness was produced.... in Ontario almost all socialists lost their deposits."

The only reason the federal conservative party didn't take power in the August 10 elections was that the Liberal Party presented itself as the most conservative party on the ballot, "which it was, in fact.

"The Liberal Party presented itself as the party of the status quo. It was this security, this immobility, which was right for an electorate which was a victim of doubts about the competence of a sovereign people.

"But there was a second factor... the electorate saw the federal elections a bit like a race where the most important thing is to bet on the winning horse."

The Liberal Party also possessed "extraordinary flexibility" which allowed it to present iself to voters as sometimes supporting change, sometimes the status quo. "They continue to vigorously apply the known word of command: 'I'm their leader, so I'd better follow them'."

The conservatives were in sad shape. Many of their traditional supporters had gone over to the Liberal Party and its future seemed doubtful. The socialist CCF was not much better off. No one wanted to vote for it during times of plenty.

But it was clear that "if the Canadian economy was struck by a grave crisis, there would be social upheavals ruinous for the old parties. But let's put things at their best: let's hope that new techniques of macro-economic stabilization and the competence of our federal civil service will spare us from those upheavals."

In 1953, the Liberal Party was filling a vacuum. "But this party of the status quo will soon be impotent in resolving . . . the drama which is forming now between the proletarian masses who are organizing to take a larger part of common wealth, and the privileged groups who will tirelessly refuse to restrict the area of their economic domination.

"I would like nationalists and socialists to draw up a concrete program of political action. . . . I would like, for example, to see them discuss together the problem of the exploitation of national resources for the benefit of the country. Perhaps they would be astonished to see at what point their ideas marry up and how convergent their means of action should be.

"I'm not under any illusions about the chances of success. But isn't the lesson of August 10, 1953, that it's extremely urgent to try the confrontation?"[4]

Trudeau picked up on his ideas of "new techniques of macro-economic stabilization" in Cité Libre the following March with an article called "Economic Fluctuations and Methods of Stabilization".

He traced economic cycles in Canada over a 60-year period and thought it would be useful to outline some ways in which the crests and troughs of the fluctuation could be smoothed out and unemployment decreased.

"Since neither individuals themselves, nor the economic system itself, can remedy the fluctuations, we're forced—whether we like it or not—to turn to the State. How can it guarantee that distributed purchasing power will transform itself completely into effective demand for produced goods?

"The most obvious solution would be to redistribute income equally among social classes, so that the poor would have more to spend, and the rich less to save. Doubtless, this method of intensifying global demand is fairly radical; though I hasten to add that it exists elsewhere!

"Firstly, since prosperity and full employment would be based on increased consumption and investment, let's see how the State can act to increase investment."

The central bank could buy back its bonds from the public, which would give the holders cash to spend. It would also substantially increase the public's deposits in banks, who would in turn lower their interest rates. The lower rates would induce businessmen to invest more. But this method alone wasn't enough to stabilize the economy because the government repurchasing of bonds didn't produce immediate results.

"At this moment, to fill the void, the government should feel obliged to increase its expenditures, be it in State enterprises (railroads, airports, canals, television etc.), or be it in public works (libraries, schools, parks and the rest)."

It was a "sad truth" that war usually imposed full employment on a country. "But perhaps the world will one day understand that it would be better to fill the void in global demand by distributing purchasing power to starving countries rather than make war on them."

Even that solution wasn't instantaneous, however. But there was one which could be administered "at the first sign of national economic weakness: that's to stimulate buying by putting more money in the hands of consumers. The State should distribute, extensively and resolutely, payments of all kinds: direct aid, unemployment insurance, agricultural assistance, various grants.

"At the same time, it should reduce taxes, to leave more money in the hands of the consumer (as well as the producer)."

Some might object that these methods were mutually opposed —how did one spend more while reducing taxes?

"The answer is quite simple: the State will have budgetary

deficits and finance itself through loans ... in practice, that will be done through the intermediary of the Bank of Canada which will open a credit account in the name of the government in return for loan certificates. (If the Bank doesn't have enough currency in circulation, it could always print some without any inconvenience when needed.)

"That will evidently scandalize those orthodox thinkers who deem intolerable a government which deliberately puts itself in debt. But if you want to smooth out economic cycles, you must distinguish between national accounting and that of a grocery store, and understand that a country isn't ruined merely because it has lent itself a lot of money."

That was a solution to unemployment and deflation. For inflation, "the government should set in motion all those mechanisms opposite to the ones described above ... in summary, it should put more money into its coffers than it takes out."

Economic science might not be perfect, but it did have these mechanisms to offer which could reduce hurtful economic cycles.

"Only, governments and citizens must not be afraid to use them."

That same spring Trudeau's wanderlust surfaced again and he decided to go to another international conference overseas—but this one was much more conventional than the one in Moscow in 1952. It was the Commonwealth Relations Conference in Lahore, Pakistan from March 17 to 28. The Canadian delegation, in which he was included, was a far cry from the one two years earlier.

The delegation's members were: Edgar McInnis, the president of the Canadian Institute of International Affairs; George Brown, a professor of history at the University of Toronto; Patrick Reid, from the department of external affairs and son of Escott, the Canadian High Commissioner to India; Ronald S. Ritchie, an economist with the Imperial Oil Company in Toronto; Frank Peers, of the Canadian Broadcasting Corporation and Ewen R. Irvine, an associate editor of the Montreal Star.

The leader of the delegation was a Toronto lawyer and Conservative member of parliament named Roland Michener. The next time Michener and Trudeau were to spend any length of time together, Michener would be governor general and Trudeau would be prime minister, 14 years later.

It was a prestigious conference, with garden parties at the prime minister's residence and royal receptions in palace parks. The conference organizers tried to maintain a relaxed atmosphere by allowing time for dances and leisure, but there were even then profound, strong undercurrents of tension in the Commonwealth.

India and Pakistan had bloodied each other only six years before in a conflict marked by atrocities on both sides. The Union of South Africa and the Federation of Rhodesia and Nyasaland were torn by racial tensions. In fact race relations were considered such an important topic, that the conference devoted one of its round table discussion groups to it.

Delegates were put up in two colonial relics, Faletti's and Nedou's hotels and trooped to the former's conference room at nine sharp each morning for the day's discussions.

Michener recalled Trudeau as being "very retiring at the conference. He was there to listen. He didn't really get involved." His wife found Trudeau "very charming. He has an almost unique understanding of women. He was never condescending. I talked to him in French as I do to anyone I meet who speaks French." Years later Trudeau would remind Mrs. Michener, "You were the only one in Lahore who spoke to me in French."

Trudeau got together with Peers and took him to the home of the regional engineer for the railroad in Lahore, whom he had met six years before during his world trip.

Peers remembers the atmosphere well. He, Trudeau and the engineer sat in his living room to talk about changes in Pakistan, while the women in the household, in purdah, waited elsewhere. The only time they entered the room was to serve tea.

The round table on race relations produced some seemingly clairvoyant statements. The Nationalist Party in South Africa, backed by the Afrikaaner, had come to power in 1948 and instituted a policy of separating the races, calling it "differential development".

A British delegate opened the discussion by "underlining the oppressive reality of the South African dilemma".

There were two roads open to them. "One was the policy of racial separation carried to its logical conclusion in the creation of separate states; the other, partnership between the races.

"Criticisms of the actual policy of the South African government came from all parts of the Commonwealth"—except Trudeau. He alone remained "deliberately aloof on the ground that the problems of South Africa were so complex and difficult that an outsider could sympathize but not criticize or venture to recommend what course should be pursued".[5]

William Clark, the diplomatic correspondent of the Observer and member of the United Kingdom's delegation, recalls agreeing with Trudeau on the issue.

"I recall an argument about this with Hugh Gaitskell, Patrick Gordon Walker and Pierre Trudeau . . . I think Mr. Trudeau was on my side in thinking that the people on the spot would have to settle the terms on which black and white lived together. . . . In this sense, I believe, Mr. Trudeau did think South Africans (of both races) should be 'left alone to solve their own problems'."

Just before Trudeau had left for the conference another one of his projects had been realized. He had been retained as the legal advisor to the Quebec Federation of Industrial Unions, the only union in the province formally affiliated with the socialist CCF (the party's Quebec wing was known as the Social Democratic Party).

The QFIU submitted a brief to a provincial royal commission March 10, which was largely written by Trudeau for the federation. He later quoted the brief's position on the division of fiscal powers between the federal and provincial governments in Cité Libre in October.

During that summer there were rumblings in Quebec about the imminent emergence of a new political party on the provincial scene, a "workers' party". But union congresses rejected the idea because they thought a class-based party would scare away too many people and, in any case, it wouldn't be able to marshal enough resources to fight a respectable election campaign.

They still wanted another party, however, as they had no use for Duplessis' party, not much more for the opposition Liberals who were considered a "corrupt, old party," and little for the CCF.

There was another centre of opposition to Duplessis in those months—a new Montreal weekly was being put together with the backing of Langevin (who had bankrolled Jean-Louis Gagnon's wartime broadcasts for the provincial Liberals) and the editing and writing ability of Jaques Hébert, a friend of Trudeau and another world traveller.

Vrai hit the stands for the first time in September and a month later carried a report on the fourth party movement.

"In several months you're going to see the Catholic Labour Confederation of Canada and the Canadian Labour Congress each hire a man to involve himself with politics in the province. The following names are being talked about: Pierre Trudeau, a brillant lawyer and reputed economist; Michel Chartrand, an old CCF candidate in Longueil ... ; Jean-Robert Ouellet, a union business agent in Shawinigan ... and a man named Daigle, an organizer for the CLCC in Sorel."

As soon as the two labour bodies had picked their men, "you will see various associations meeting and forming political committees, first in Shawinigan, Arvida, Asbestos ... these political committees will issue cards to members. Those who want one will have to make regular contributions; they should also participate in frequent study sessions to prepare a program and revise it as needed."

As it turned out, nothing came of the idea, but it formed the basis of another movement two years later, which Trudeau was to help found.

While that project lost its momentum and died, another succeeded, mainly through groundwork by Maurice Lamontagne. For several years he had been attending the annual Couchiching conferences of the Canadian Institute of Public Affairs. The institute was oriented toward English Canada and Lamontagne lamented the fact there was no French Canadian equivalent. "The solitudes existed even in those days," he later said. So he gathered together his friends from Cité Libre, the social reform group at Laval University, Le Devoir, the CCF and Liberal parties and the University of Montreal.

"Our prime purpose was to meet and discuss our political freedom," explained Lamontagne.

The group met in the plush Windsor Hotel in Montreal in early September, 1954 and planned the first meeting of the Institut Canadien des Affaires Publiques and its organization.

Léon Lortie, an official at the University of Montreal, was made president. Trudeau, Lamontagne and Marcel Faribault were made vice-presidents. The secretary-treasurer was a federal Liberal party organizer in Quebec, Louis de Gonzague (Bob) Giguère. Among the members of the executive were Gerard Pelletier, Charles Lussier, Jean-Louis Gagnon, and Edmond Labelle, who had been in Paris with Trudeau.

The first meeting was held in the Alpine Inn in Ste. Marguerite, from September 29 to October 2 when Gagnon, Pelletier, Jean Marchand and Trudeau all gave papers on "The Sovereign People".

Trudeau's paper was above all a warning. It was read last at the meeting, addressed to "citizens" and told them of obstacles to democracy in Quebec.

Reminding them that the price of liberty was eternal vigilance, Trudeau said: "Citizens should never stop perfecting the institutions by which they govern themselves, nor cease to adapt them to the demands of the continually changing society of man. Thus it is to respond to the needs of a growing population or increasing territory that new ways of representation have to be found. To control a bureaucratic invasion, administration has to be decentralized and the role of parliamentary committees accentuated. To prevent political equality being rendered inoperable by the sole fact of economic inequality, social legislation has to be widened.

"If citizens lose, for one moment, the control of their governmental machines, or if they let events pass them by, they will be swiftly engulfed by storms of despotism and anarchy."

Obstacles to democracy were everywhere to be found. "In a great neighboring country we see the freedom of thought dangerously beaten down. . . . Our own national state is also guilty of inadmissible blows to civil liberties: need we be reminded of the suppression of Habeas Corpus and imprisonment without trial during the last war? Or the ignoble treatment inflicted on Canadians of Japanese origin? Or this parody of justice that was called an inquiry into espionage?"[6]

Turning to his province, he said "I submit that the particular political difficulties in Quebec have developed because our population arrived at the stage of an established democracy without ever having to fight for it."

One result was that "we never ceased complaining to Providence to give us some 'chiefs': we have always conceived of action as being the function of elites.

"Isn't it the truth that individually, we never learned to love liberty? And don't the obstacles to democracy in our province come from the fact that we don't really believe in popular sovereignty?

"Isn't our lack of passion for individual liberty the result of our ideologies, institutions and even our environment teaching us to obey, but rarely to command? . . . our young people from the country spend the winter in shipyards to breathe the air of freedom; but they only escape family discipline and the protection of priests to fall under the hands of foreign foremen . . . We townspeople take our places in the authoritative structures of capitalism; we live there in the fear of being thrown out on the street, be it through crises of the system or be it by the bosses who are always English . . .

"Is it still possible to overturn these obstacles? . . . the time that's left is short."

The fall of 1954 was notable for one other occurrence: Trudeau found himself siding with Duplessis in a federal-provincial confrontation.

The federal Liberal government had offered a subsidy to Quebec for its universities but Duplessis had rejected it firmly September 15, arguing that education was an entirely provincial matter as outlined in the British North America Act.

Trudeau declared his agreement publicly when he wrote an open letter to his friend Jacques Hébert, the editor of Vrai,

suggesting that Duplessis should be congratulated "for his opposition in principle to federal meddling in the provincial do-
main".

Trudeau continued, however, to suggest that Duplessis give
his opposition a more "inventive turn" which would aid the
cause of French Canadianism at the same time.

He wanted Duplessis to accept the two million dollar subsidy
and apply it to universities, as that was the stipulation. At the
same time, however, and with a great deal of publicity, the
Quebec Government should channel exactly the same amount of
money into separate schools, bonuses to federal civil servants
who could pass a French language proficiency test, and a service
to make bilingual plaques and install them in federal buildings,
embassies and federal transport (Trans Canada Airlines and Canadian National Railways).

This policy would serve three ends, said Trudeau. It would
underline Duplessis' opposition to federal meddling, prevent two
million dollars being returned to the federal government for its
use and "furnish precious aid to the French Canadian culture".

"I assure you, my dear Jacques, that my plan is very realistic
and basically very serious . . .

"Think about it. One year, an office would be opened in
Ottawa offering, let's say, $100 to any federal civil servant who
succeeded in proving his knowledge of French. The next year,
the same could be done for Canadian military personnel in
every city where there is a garrison. Yet another year, you and I
could leave to nail bilingual plaques on all our embassies in the
world."

After this sally, his life was low key for the next two years
except for a short article, almost an aside, which went back to
Father Braun.

On March 3, 1955, the Soviets had expelled Father Bisson-
nette, an American member of the Assumptionist Order, who
had been serving in Moscow, the same job Braun had done for
12 years.

"One hopes he will be less garrulous than one of his predeces-
sors, Father Léopold Braun. That one prided himself in being
very useful to the anti-Soviet cause by gathering information in

Moscow on behalf of the Americans. And even a long while after his return from the U.S.S.R., one heard mysteriously that he kept 'sources and means of information on current events in the communist world'.

"If some high priest of Buddhism or an orthodox religion came to Canada under the cover of religion, and after having left our country publicly prided himself with his connivances with enemies of the Canadian government, we would have soon put his fellow-men out the door or in prison. And we would have been right.

"Whereas with the communists . . . "[8]

The following year, 1956, was eventful for the communist world. Three years after the death of Stalin, the new Soviet regime was beginning a "de-Stalinization program". There were flare-ups in Poland and Czechoslovakia and a full-scale revolt in Hungary which was brutally put down by Mongolian troops flown across Russia for that express purpose.

The Suez Canal was seized by a combined force of British and French troops and Canada's external affairs minister, Lester Bowles Pearson, won a Nobel Peace Prize for his mediation efforts in the dispute.

In Canada as well, events were turbulent. Duplessis had called an election for June 20 and the opposition Liberal and CCF parties were gearing up for another attempt to unseat him.

Trudeau and several friends met twice before the election, in April and June, to decide whether or not they should try to launch a new anti-Duplessis movement or party. They chose not to, and confined themselves to running as candidates or campaigning for other candidates.

Trudeau decided to support the CCF and made speeches in Sorel for Jean-Paul Geoffroy, in Rouyn-Noranda for Jean-Robert Ouellette and for Pierre Vadboncoeur in Beloeuil.

Vadboncoeur recalls that they had arranged to speak in a rented parish hall, but the priest refused at the last moment, so "Trudeau gave his speech from the back of a truck over a loudspeaker. There was only a handful of people there, some women with baby carriages and some small boys on their bicycles honking their horns." With them was Thérèse Casgrain, Quebec secretary of the CCF.

Michel Chartrand remembers yet another speech in Mc-Masterville, when there weren't enough people to fill the parish hall and once again Trudeau spoke from the back of the truck. "We didn't worry about the number of people there," said Chartrand of the few that were present. "We were advocating socialism." Later Trudeau told Chartrand, "Michel, there is no other way out for minorities, we French Canadians, than socialism".

At that time Chartrand thought of Trudeau as a Fabian socialist. "He was against capitalism."

Vadboncoeur's success at the polls, despite Trudeau's efforts, was indicative of the CCF's as a whole.

"At the first radio reports I was quite dispirited because I had only received eight votes. I said to myself, not even my friends are voting for me." He received a total of 33 votes.

The election's results were as Trudeau had predicted several years before—Duplessis once more was carried to victory.

It was after this election victory, Duplessis' fifth, that Trudeau and some close associates got down to the serious business of founding a new political movement.

FOOTNOTES CHAPTER 6

1. Relations, November, 1952.
2. Pierre Elliott Trudeau, "Réflexions sur la politique au Canada francais," Cité Libre, December, 1952.
3. Cité Libre, May, 1953.
4. Pierre Elliott Trudeau, "L'Élection Fédérale; Prodromes et Conjectures," Cité Libre, November, 1953.
5. "The Multi-Racial Commonwealth," The Royal Institute of International Affairs, London, 1955.
6. At the start of the Second World War the federal government enforced the Defence of Canada Regulations to summarily intern persons supporting communism or fascism. After Russia was invaded and joined the Allies, the communists were released. The espionage inquiry Trudeau refers to appears to be the royal com-

mission of inquiry into the revelations of Igor Gouzenko, the Soviet cypher clerk who defected in September, 1945 with documents exposing a spy ring for the Soviets, involving many Canadian communists including a member of parliament, Fred Rose.

7. Vrai, December 11, 1954.

8. Pierre Elliott Trudeau, "Les Deux Mesures," Cité Libre, May, 1955.

7

Political Action

Le Rassemblement was the fruit of the halting, tentative steps taken two years earlier, in 1954, by two labour federations to start a new political party. As Vrai had then noted, Trudeau's name was one mentioned in connection with the attempt.

On April 14 he met with Pierre Dansereau, the dean of the faculty of social science at the University of Montreal, Thérèse Casgrain, Jacques Perrault, Laurendeau of Le Devoir and Pelletier. The group decided it was too late to create a strong centre of opposition to Duplessis but agreed to continue working toward creating one.

They worked over the summer and Le Rassemblement was born September 8 at its founding convention. About 100 people attended, officers were elected and the constitution adopted.

Dansereau was made first president, a move which he said made Duplessis try to get him fired. The "movement for education and democratic action" was "open to all people of democratic persuasions, except those belonging to an undemocratic party," he said.

"There was only one political party that was democratic—the CCF. Trudeau was absolutely adamant about not admitting Lamontagne and Gagnon because they were members of the Liberal Party."

Gagnon remembers that well. "I wrote a letter asking if I could join Le Rassemblement but Trudeau and Pelletier told me they didn't want any Liberals." He still has the $3 money order for membership that was returned to him. Gagnon didn't think the movement really had that much relevance, even in 1956. "Duplessis was getting older and the Liberals were getting stronger.

"Trudeau just couldn't get used to the idea of joining a political party. I believe he was looking for a way to become a power in the land without joining a political party."

If he was trying to become "a power in the land" he started on the right foot by surrounding himself with dynamic personalities. Some of the members of Le Rassemblement were: René Lévesque; Jacques-Yvan Morin; Jean-Luc Pépin; Jean-Pierre Goyer; Jacques Hébert; Gerard Pelletier; Dansereau; Laurendeau; Robert Bourassa; Casgrain; Jerome Choquette and Gerard Filion.

Trudeau was elected vice-president and Morin, Pelletier, Laurendeau, Hébert and Arture Tremblay were all elected to the executive.

He helped write the constitution which embodied this general principle: "A true political conscience will be born only at the instigation of a vast political education movement which will make the people conscious of their powers and put them in a well-established position to exercise them."

All Quebecers who were interested in "building a truly democratic society" were invited to join the movement. Four months later, it counted about 250 members in four or five major centres around the province.

Some of Le Rassemblement's specific principles had the ring of Trudeau's earlier Cité Libre articles.

"The goal of all economic activity being the satisfaction of human needs, it follows that society should organize itself to draw from available resources the best results possible for the whole of the population.

"A human economy should abolish the exploitation of man by man and share production increases and leisure equally among citizens.

"This result will be attained by: the stabilization of employment at the highest possible level; the best possible utilization of natural resources; the putting to work of appropriate technology to ensure the greatest possible production and the most equal distribution possible of the fruits and burdens of economic activity among all members collectively.

"In the scheme of production, private initiative and property, collective initiative and co-operative property, public initiative and nationalization, are only *means* in the service of human and economic objectives, and should be evaluated as such.

"It's impossible to predict precisely which ideal economic structures must be put in place... Meanwhile, in our highly industrialized societies, private initiative left to itself cannot guarantee common prosperity. That must be assured through planning."

The principles also advocated assured, stable markets for farmers and craftsmen, the right to work guaranteed, just remuneration for work and a move toward industrial democracy to prevent "the dehumanization of work as a consequence of industrialization".

Le Rassemblement never became a mass movement, in fact its membership never exceeded 600, but it did group together academics, intellectuals, union officials and the press in an open, free-wheeling atmosphere.

It should not be seen, however, as solely a parochial, inward-looking, Quebec-oriented movement. While its emphasis was on the provincial scene, it also recognized as a principle that "whatever the motives are that lead men to group themselves into distinct societies, the ultimate allegiance of each is to the human race. Men of all countries are dependent upon each other and in time of need they should help each other with brotherly aid."

Trudeau himself picked up on this theme when he spoke to more than 100 University of Montreal students at a meeting of the International Relations Club in October, about the time of his thirty-seventh birthday.

Political maturity and well-defined political thought were needed to understand and appreciate international events as well as provincial ones, Trudeau said.

It was particularly necessary to avoid "poisonous nationalism whose passions and feelings prevent the tackling of problems rationally".

This was why, provincially, French Canadians elected someone who claimed to protect "our race and our autonomy" without considering problems of corruption and a weakened economy etc. In Ottawa they elected Louis St. Laurent, merely because he was a French Canadian who would protect their interests.

"And finally, on the international scene, they [French Canadians] oppose the recognition of communist China, because they have already had missionaries who have been badly treated there or because the United States doesn't want to, without considering that the present government of Mao Tse-tung has ruled a quarter of the world's population for the past five years."[1]

Trudeau then attended the annual general meeting of the provincial Liberal Party on October 19 and 20 both as an observer, and as a reporter for Jacques Hébert's newspaper, Vrai.

He had few kind words for them.

"The Congress of the provincial Liberal Federation ... let me measure two things: on one hand, the desolating sterility of three quarters of a century of Liberal partisanship, and on the other the courageous attempts at renewal by a handful of militants."

While the theme of the Congress was "The Future of the Liberal Party," it seemed to be stuck in the past. Paul Gérin-Lajoie, the principal speaker, "found it useful to devote a good third of his speech to evoking 'glorious Liberal traditions.'

"However I can't help but admire the tenacity of a small group of men who are undertaking to infuse some democratic blood into the veins of a party which has never been anything but a coterie of vested interests. It's tempting to tell them, 'It's not worth it. These transfusions will quickly bleed you white and won't help to bring an already rotting cadaver back to life ...'

"But ... it must be recognized that in this fight against death, they haven't lost the first round. The Liberal machine, I mean the small group of finance and reaction, hasn't succeeded in killing the Federation.

"But without doubt, the most important event in these two days was the appearance of Jean-Louis Gagnon. Many hoped that the defeat in the last election would serve to balance off this 'red' ... but the opposite happened.

"In the only speech really looking to the future, and with a vigour of attack unseen in these circles, Gagnon literally galvanized a Congress which until then had been petty and quibbling."[2]

Shortly afterward, Trudeau wrote that "democratic renewal in our province should develop outside existing parties. . . . and that is why I belong to Le Rassemblement.

"That's also the bet of a growing number of citizens who refuse to believe that there's only one way of getting into politics: by entering one of the old parties and 'changing it from the inside.' By believing this myth, successive generations have seen their energy and political sincerity annihilated. We find it's essential to look elsewhere in the future."[3]

That autumn in 1956 was also notable for another event, which although not overtly political, was nevertheless prodoundly so: the publication of a book of essays edited by Trudeau called The Asbestos Strike.

The book was the child of five years of labour, fathered by Frank R. Scott of McGill University, who had been involved with the group of young intellectuals, labour leaders and academics in the strike seven years earlier.

"We were all convinced that this event marked a turning point in the social history of Quebec," said Scott, and he decided it had to be chronicled.

The project needed time and money, and Scott arranged for the latter. Alan Plaunt, an old Canadian socialist friend whom Scott had met decades before at Oxford University, had come into $200,000 in the thirties. Plaunt, with Graham Spry, were the prime movers in founding the government-owned Canadian Broadcasting Corporation. When he died, his wife offered the interest from the estate to Scott to finance any projects he thought socially worthwhile and he formed the Recherches Sociales group to utilize the money.

In the early fifties Scott contacted Gerard Pelletier, the editor of the CLCC newspaper, Le Travail, and he produced an outline for the proposed book. Jean Gérin-Lajoie, an official with the United Steelworkers of America, was assigned the task of editing the book, but was later replaced by Trudeau. Jean-Charles Falardeau, a professor of the faculty of social sciences at Laval University, advised Scott and helped him with the overall planning of the book.

As it turned out, the book was virtually a product of the Cité Libre group – five of the nine authors were: Trudeau; Pelletier; Jean-Paul Geoffroy; Charles Lussier and Reginald Boisvert.

There was also Gilles Beausoleil, an economist, Fernand Dumont, a professor in the same faculty as Falardeau, Maurice Sauvé, an advisor to the National Metal Trades Federation and Gerard Dion. Dion had made his name in July, 1956, when he co-authored with another abbé, Louis O'Neill, an explosive book called "Political Immorality in the Province of Quebec" which had sold more than 100,000 copies.

All was not sweetness and light in the production of the book. There was tension between Trudeau and Falardeau because Trudeau belittled both the role and importance of Falardeau's colleague Georges-Henri Lévesque and the faculty of social science at Laval which he had founded.

Trudeau wrote the introductory chapter and epilogue to the book. Falardeau found them "too bitter". Nevertheless he described Trudeau's contribution as being "a document of rare candour" and "nimbly sketched".

Trudeau's old friend, André Laurendeau, was more critical when he reviewed his chapters in Le Devoir.

Trudeau's opening chapter, giving the historical background of Quebec at the time of the strike, was not history, but polemics.

"The writer wields a wicked blade that flashes and whistles through the air with lethal precision and leaves a trail of severed heads behind it . . .

"He is a French Canadian deceived by his own kind...I think he is ashamed to have had such ancestors."

His thesis was summarized by Laurendeau this way: "By their prejudice and ignorance in socio-economic matters, Quebec nationalists have long prevented their intellectual elite from seeing the dramatic changes that our people were living through, changes which amount to a real industrial revolution. When they did happen to recognize certain features of this change, the same prejudices and the same incompetence prevented them from proposing viable solutions to the problems it raised."[4]

Trudeau himself saw a historical inevitability about the strike. "History knows no abrupt turns; the forces at work in the present have arisen in the past...For many people, however, the drama at Asbestos was a violent announcement that a new era had begun...For them, this strike is a turning point in the entire religious, political, social and economic history of the Province of Quebec."

Here was a province whose population, in the first half of the twentieth century, had increased by 136 per cent and migrated en masse to the cities where over half of them were paid substandard wages in primary and secondary industry.

The whole environment of Quebec society was traditionalist and imbued with "fuzzy thinking". The French Canadian clergy "were scarcely willing to recognize the advent of industrialization and the conversion of the masses into a proletariat".

The Church's opinions on politics were hardly progressive. In 1939, Cardinal Villeneuve had said that the socialist "CCF differs from communism mainly in that it does not seek to obtain its ends by violent means" and that "fascism has made a great contribution to saving the peace of Europe".

The strongest agent of change in Quebec had been the Catholic French Canadian trade unions which had helped develop "working-class consciousness," although "this result was a chance by-product".

One group connected with the review L'Action Francaise had spoken of the urgent need for economic nationalism in a series of articles in the mid-1920s.

Commenting, Trudeau wrote: "The common good would

doubtless have been better served if our researchers had studied the unequal distribution of our provincial wealth less from the ethnic point of view and more from the point of view of social classes and the inequities inherent in economic liberalism. To do so, however, they would have had to attack the economic dictatorship with more vigour and to devote to real reforms of structure (teaching, nationalization, planned economy, etc.) some of the energy that was lavished on nationalism.

"Figures suggest that financial and social status are of prime importance in determining access to university studies. The great majority of children born into poor families, then, must be satisfied with a few years of primary school, where their readers and their arithmetic problems extoll the bourgeois values and illustrate the glories of the free enterprise system."

Of all the organizations and institutions in French Canada, the unions were by far the most important. "The 'list of demands' of any labour union one cares to name has done more to influence the destinies of our changing society than all the libraries filled by our official social thinkers."

Trudeau concluded his opening chapter by saying that the wage-earning and salaried workers "counted for almost nothing in our social thought, our Church, our institutions devoted to teaching and propaganda, our national societies, our political parties, our deliberative assemblies, or the legislative and executive branches of government".

The strike was significant because "it occurred at a time when we were witnessing the passing of a world, precisely at a moment when our social framework – the worm-eaten remnants of a bygone age – was ready to come apart".

What could one look forward to in the future? There was some hope that groups of nationalists would move to the left. In September, 1953, Jean-Marc Léger, a Cité Libriste, had written an article in L'Action Nationale, a nationalist review, "bringing the solutions of socialism to the attention of his readers".

"It is this courage and lucidity in certain fields which inspire the occasional hope that some of these nationalists will one day come to realize that they will only be able to make the transition from the past to the future by means of social radicalism."

Unions had shown more and more promise after the strike. The CLCC had formed a political action committee and the Quebec Federation of Industrial Unions, at its 1954 congress, "moved toward a more effective political action" and the most dynamic elements in this movement came to advocate that the progressive political forces be brought together in the bosom of a new left.

"Our society, then, is in a state of unstable equilibrium, based on a present state of things which is torn between opposing lines of force."

There was going to be strong opposition to any change. "Behind the solid ramparts of the police and a certain theology the propertied class is cleverly working to adorn the old system of ownership with new and less provocative finery.

"We no longer live in a static world: we must go forward with the caravan of humanity or perish in the desert of time past. The current developments in technology and politics herald a future social and industrial revolution in comparison with which the previous one will seem but child's play."

There were several traditional ideas that needed revision because of their "very debilitating effect on our capacity to adapt ourselves to the transformations of the future, and to become masters of it.

"Our social philosophy, for example, recognizes as proprietors only those who – today the holders of a stock – will trade it tomorrow on the stock exchange . . . "

But on the other hand, "workers who have invested the best years of their lives, their greatest efforts, and their finest hopes in a job or a profession, are not to have any property rights over this occupation, and may find themselves *expropriated without compensation* with the onset of a strike, a lockout, a business recession, or simply old age."

Another idea that needed revision, held by "small-time moralists", was that workers should have no share in management.

"Not satisfied with opposing *industrial* democracy, they look with great disfavour upon any desire of the working class to play an effective role, at last in *political* democracy . . .

"Clearly, when the revolution produced by automation, cybernetics, and nuclear energy has completely altered the foundations of the present regime of property and authority; when a certain amount of state planning has become an absolute necessity for controlling the chaotic conditions of the period of transition and when the nationalization of the principal means of production has become an established fact, there will still be clerics around to proclaim, with an old text of Pius XI in hand, that the social doctrine of the Church has never ceased to be avant-garde.

"Let us bear clearly in mind that there is no question here of proclaiming a new regime of industrial liberty, nor of advocating socialism, still less of sketching an economic theory of plenty for all. It is simply a matter of prosaically applying the lessons of the last fifty years to the present."

Trudeau's last sentence of the book read, "Who will reproach us because we still believe, with the labour movement as a whole, in the promise: Blessed are those who hunger and thirst for righteousness, for they shall be satisfied?"[5]

Trudeau may have meant the question rhetorically, but within two months a reproach did come in the form of a book by Robert Rumilly. It proved to be the single most extensive, profound, damaging attack thus far on the beliefs and structures of Trudeau and his friends.

Rumilly's small paperback, "The Leftist Infiltration of French Canada," exploded on the Quebec scene shortly before Christmas, 1956.

In 147 pages of detailed documentation, Rumilly exposed what he believed was an insidious, well-managed network dedicated to socialism and the destruction of the authority of the Church and the State.

At the centre of this network he placed Pierre Elliott Trudeau.

In French Canada, Rumilly was a heavyweight, a formidable adversary.

A member of the elite, prestigious Académie Canadienne-Francaise, he had written a 41-volume history of Quebec, an 800-page biography of a famous French Canadian, Henri Bourassa, and other historical works.

Still vigorous and incisive at 60, Rumilly was an unrepentant right-winger, a Catholic of the old school and an ardent French Canadian nationalist.

The tone of his book is bitter and outraged, but that is perhaps understandable.

Rumilly, born in Martinique in 1897, spent his next few years in French Indochina before moving to Metropolitan France with his family.

After an uneventful childhood he fought in the Great War, not from any particular dislike for the Germans, he says, but for a taste of adventure. But after the war life altered radically for Robert Rumilly.

"The class warfare was awful. Because I was a bourgeois intellectual with glasses I wasn't able to sit beside a taxi driver who was considered part of the working class."[6]

Class warfare increased with left-wing power until Rumilly could stand it no longer and he fled to French Canada in 1927.

But in the early fifties in Quebec, he perceived the same trends developing that had driven him from France.

To Rumilly the trend wasn't simply a distant ideology or academic theory. It was a painful, and perhaps eventually fatal, infection in the body of his adopted country.

The infection was a network that comprised Cité Libre, the Canadian Broadcasting Corporation's French service—Radio-Canada, Le Devoir, L'Institut Canadien des Affaires Publiques, Vrai and Le Rassemblement.

He saw the six elements of this network supporting, feeding and defending each other.

Of the six, Trudeau had helped found three and was a contributor to the other three.

Deliberately, Rumilly opened his book not with Canadians or their groups, but with a long chapter on the French movement, "Catholics of the Left".

" 'Catholics of the Left' shake their fists at the right, where the great majority of catholics are found, and offer their hands to the communists, for whom they have complete complaisance," wrote Rumilly.[7]

These catholics considered communists as "brothers a little more advanced, as avant-garde, with whom they will join before too long". They admitted they found certain faults in communism, unhappily, but also a lot of good.

Rumilly linked several Catholics of the Left with communist causes in France. One was Jean-Marie Domenach, the editor-in-chief of Esprit and Trudeau's friend.

He recalled a demonstration organized by French communists in 1952 against the American general, Matthew Bunker Ridgway, which was banned because of threatened violence.

A handful of French intellectuals, Domenach among them, signed a petition protesting the ban which was published in L'Humanité, the communist party newspaper.

Rumilly then cited several passages from Esprit, which to him were convincing proof of where the review and Catholics of the Left stood politically.

June, 1945: "Never, under any pretext, will we participate in any anti-communist front: anti-communism is virtual or declared treason."

October, 1946: Esprit's publisher and founder, Emmanuel Mounier, wrote, "a Christian can adopt most political positions of communism and conclude alliances with it".

October, 1947: Jean-Louis Lévy wrote, "Capitalism is condemned to death and knows it . . . Triumphant American capitalism has a bad conscience, the entire world's bourgeois class has a bad conscience, and is afraid. As for communism, it doesn't need war to develop, for time works for it."

Capitalism's struggle is "chaotic and self-devouring" while communism is a "constructive and harmonious system", continued Lévy.

Even priests got into the act. He quoted a Dominican, the Reverend Father Henri-Charles Desroches, who wrote an article entitled "Marxism and Religion" in the May-June edition of Esprit in 1948.

Rumilly said the thesis of Desroches, in his own words, was: "It's possible for believers to profit from Marxism."

Tongue in cheek, Rumilly recounted one last example from Esprit.

"The February, 1949 edition protested against the municipal councillors of Paris who wanted to change the name of the subway station 'Stalingrad'. (This was before the de-Stalinization program in Moscow!)"

Rumilly was not alone in his opposition to Catholics of the Left, also called Progressive Christians. He quoted L'Osservatore Romano, the Vatican's official organ, as saying March 5, 1949 of their flirtation with communism:

"Progressive Christians risk being taken in by a doctrine condemned by the Church and contributing to the success of a party systematically anti-Christian and aggressive."

Having outlined the ideas of the Catholics of the Left as he saw them, Rumilly described the leftist network, starting with Cité Libre, the review Trudeau helped found and co-directed.

Cité Libre started in Europe, said Rumilly, when Canadian students were indoctrinated and denationalized by Catholics of the Left in France before returning to Canada.

This cadre of students was inculcated with "a mentality of contempt and hatred, revolutionary aspirations and confused ideas where class struggle played a large role".

This cadre founded Cité Libre, which was modelled on Esprit. In fact, Rumilly noted, Cité Libre called itself the "little sister" of Esprit.

In essence, Cité Libre was leftist, anti-church and anti-authority.

Trudeau, "the Moscow pilgrim" as Rumilly called him, was quoted from an article he wrote in Cité Libre.

"There's no divine right for prime ministers any more than there is for bishops. They don't have any more authority over us than we want them to have."

In response to Trudeau, Rumilly quoted Abbé J.-B. Desrosiers, who criticized Trudeau in the January 10, 1953 edition of Nos Cours, the official organ of the Pius XI Institute in Montreal.

"This brief passage," wrote Desrosiers, "contains the substance of communism, because it undermines the social order."

Rumilly then recalled the special edition of Esprit, in the summer of 1952, which was dedicated to French Canada and edited and written by Cité Libristes.

Henri-Irenée Marrou, a professor of history at the Sorbonne, contributor to Esprit and one of France's most militant Catholics of the Left, had written the preface.

This was the same man, said Rumilly, who resigned from UNESCO as one of France's representatives to protest the admission of Spain.

"This 'Catholic of the Left' then is fairly representative: the presence of Marxist Russia appears completely natural to him, but that of Catholic Spain keeps him awake at night."

Despite the fact that this issue of Esprit was heavily criticized by the church in French Canada, Rumilly was convinced it helped launch Cité Libre. Bitterly he added:

"Rationalism and Marxism are the basic tendencies about which the editors of Cité Libre orient themselves—perhaps, in certain cases, without their knowledge."

To make matters worse, Cité Libre wasn't working in isolation.

"Each issue of Cité Libre is signalled, hailed, acclaimed in the columns of Le Devoir," he wrote, and gave several examples of fulsome praise for articles in Cité Libre and Esprit.

Rumilly was obviously a man not easily intimidated. Le Devoir may have been one of French Canada's oldest, and certainly its most influential, newspapers, but to him it was no sacred cow.

Le Devoir, said Rumilly, cynically invented or falsified news and misled the public. He gave several examples. He accused the newspaper and its editor, Gerard Filion, of fomenting hatred between workers and management. But Rumilly noted that Filion's relations with his own typesetters were far from cordial.

In the spring of 1955 they demanded a raise to bring their wages close to those of the competition. Le Devoir resisted the raise and negotiations started. But Filion was meanwhile recruiting scabs to work and when the typesetters arrived for work at 6 p.m., April 20, they were met by police who told them there was no work for them.

Some of them, said Rumilly, had worked there for 30 years.

He found suspect the fact that two contributors to Le Devoir and the editor had travelled expenses-paid behind the Iron Curtain and returned to Canada to write what he believed were favourable articles.

Again, the official church position backed up Rumilly. The Jesuit review, Relations, laid down the law thus:

"It is inadmissible for Catholics to travel behind the Iron Curtain at the expense of communist organizations. Communists are persecutors and excommunicated. If they pay for trips by Catholics, it is because they count on getting their propaganda across under a Catholic label, which would not have been acceptable if it had been presented by a communist."

Rumilly then criticized Trudeau for his 1952 Moscow trip, and Jacques Hébert for his trip to Poland at the invitation of the government and his "great praise for communist accomplishments".

Gerard Filion was also singled out for his trip to mainland China in the company of several English-speaking Canadians "all communist or communist sympathizers.

"No one is claiming that Gerard Filion was converted to communism," continued Rumilly. "But one is obliged to state his indulgence, his good-will and his complaisance for communism, like Jacques Hébert and Pierre Trudeau."

Jacques Hébert was the head of another part of the network, as publisher of the weekly tabloid Vrai.

Gilles Marcotte and Pelletier were both contributors to Vrai and Cité Libre and had also written for Le Devoir. Vrai was even printed on Le Devoir's presses.

Rumilly listed some of the active members of the Institut Canadien des Affaires Publiques, which he named as another part of the network: André Laurendeau, Gerard Filion, Gerard Pelletier, Pierre Elliott Trudeau and Jean-Louis Gagnon.

These "intellectuals of the left" invited Hubert Beuve-Méry, publisher of the Parisian paper Le Monde, and noted French leftist, to their first meeting in 1954, and another leftist, Marrou, to their annual meeting two years later.

According to an observer at a later meeting whom Rumilly quoted, the tone of the meeting was negative.

Those attending the meeting were against nationalism, against the clergy, against some parental rights in education and against a political authority they considered incompetent, inert and corrupt.

A movement similar to the institute, which added to the network, was Le Rassemblement, which Trudeau served as vice-president.

Vrai called it a "political bombshell" and Le Devoir described it as a "new political movement", but Rumilly didn't see much new in Le Rassemblement.

Its senior officers were Laurendeau, Hébert, Pelletier and the omnipresent Trudeau. [In fact, Pierre Dansereau, its president, later became president of the institute.]

"In the opera," Rumilly remarked drily, "to generate a mass effect, the producer makes the same figures march past several times. Is it to create the same effect that the members of L'Institut Canadien formed Le Rassemblement?"

The last member of the network was the most powerful simply because it had the most money—the government-owned Canadian Broadcasting Corporation.

The CBC's Radio-Canada contained a group of leftists who formed a "family compact", he said.

"At any hour of the day, the listener hears . . . the same participants, producers and commentators, and the same guests, all members of a tightly knit group. Nevertheless this group opened its ranks to the leftists from Le Devoir—Cité Libre—Vrai—L'Institut Canadien Des Affaires Publiques and Le Rassemblement."

Rumilly listed several people he considered leftists who had been featured at Radio-Canada and then asked rhetorically if the service would be so ready to offer its microphones to others who were traditionalists and nationalists.

"Even more cynical, the annual meetings of L'Institut Canadien des Affaires Publiques are organized with the co-operation, moral and financial, of Radio-Canada.

"It's with Radio-Canada money ... that Léon Lortie, Gerard Pelletier, André Laurendeau, Jean-Louis Gagnon, Pierre Elliott Trudeau and their friends are able to indoctrinate the public!"

Scarcely had Le Rassemblement been founded, when its president was invited to a Radio-Canada television show and drew "magnificent publicity," he said.

On the other hand, when he formed an opposition group, the Centre d'Information Nationale, and asked for the same treatment, his group received just enough exposure—a token, once-over-lightly effort—to let Radio-Canada say it had "played the game of impartiality".

When Albert Béguin, the publisher of Esprit, came to Canada, a press conference directed by René Lévesque and attended by Gerard Pelletier and Jean-Marc Léger was a matter of course, fumed Rumilly.

But when an eminent French Catholic of the Right visited at the same time, a friend who tried to arrange a radio interview for him was told there wasn't any time available.

"Radio-Canada, as it's now functioning, is illegal," he charged.

In Canada, educational rights were reserved for the provinces. But Radio-Canada was functioning as a vehicle for "popular education" leading French Canadians "toward an ideology contrary to their traditions and national aspirations".

Patiently, slowly, this intricate, interdependent network was striving toward two ends.

First, it was trying to substitute the idea of class and socialism for that of nationalism, which Rumilly believed were mutually exclusive.

Second, the network was attempting to pull together a popular front of leftists in French Canada to form a new political party.

The popular front, said Rumilly, was already being formed by the "fusion of the groups from Le Devoir, L'Action Nationale and Cité Libre".

That fusion should result, Léger had written, in a "French Canadian social party" which should "collaborate quite naturally on the federal scene with the CCF, the labour party of English Canada.

"It was in the summer of 1952 that Léger announced this plan. Its accomplishment, which was pursued methodically, is almost finished at the end of 1956.

"Pierre Elliott Trudeau advocated, at the congress of the Friends of Le Devoir in January, 1955, a 'socialist orientation'. Jacques Perrault, president of Le Devoir, officially belongs to the socialist party. Jean-Marc Léger and other left-wing, French Canadian theoreticians openly advocate the same membership ... Frank R. Scott [who contributed to the same special Esprit edition in 1952 as Léger], professor at McGill University, is one of the leading lights and theoreticians of the socialist party.

"Maurice Lamontagne, theoretician of centralization, was the vice-president of the Institut Canadien des Affaires Publiques. Mme. Thérèse Casgrain, head of the socialist party in Quebec, sat on the same committee."

Francine Laurendeau, the daughter of André Laurendeau and niece of Jacques Perrault, was elected the head of Socialist Youth, the youth wing of the CCF, at its convention in Winnipeg in August, 1956, noted Rumilly.

Members of the Quebec-based Social Democratic Party adopted the Winnipeg manifesto of the CCF and when Perrault returned to Quebec from the convention he "appeared on television as the spokesman of the CCF".

The danger in a French Canadian socialist party was clear to Rumilly.

"A socialist party, whatever its French Canadian label, would be the main link in a Popular Front, knowing no enemies on the left, and based on the French model.

" ... A Canadian Popular Front would embrace everyone from liberals of Jean-Louis Gagnon's persuasion to those on the extreme left," he believed.

It must have been a chilling experience for Rumilly to see an alliance suggested in Canada similar to that in France between Esprit and French communists.

He quoted an article from Combat, the official organ of the Communist Party of Quebec, on September 1, 1956.

Combat, said Rumilly, "advocated an open alliance between communists and 'Catholics of the Left' in Canada".

A clarion call and a warning concluded Rumilly's small book.

"By continuous agitation, by the harassing of provincial authority, by the tone of their arguments, by the divisions they have introduced amongst nationalists and Catholics, by the propagation of the idea of class struggle, leftists are creating a climate of civil war in the province of Quebec...

"The leftists are denationalizing our youth. In the struggle for provincial autonomy, they have formed a fifth column in the service of the enemy...

"To all those who passionately love French Canada, and fear for her future, I cry, 'Help us, now is the hour!'...

"Show to our youth that certain ideas, like certain diseases, are fatal."

FOOTNOTES CHAPTER 7

1. Quartier Latin, November 22, 1956.
2. Vrai, November 3, 1956.
3. Vrai, November 24, 1956.
4. André Laurendeau, "André Laurendeau: Witness for Quebec," articles selected and translated by Phillip Stratford, Macmillan of Canada, Toronto, 1973. The review originally appeared in three parts in Le Devoir on October 6, 10 and 11, 1956.
5. Pierre Elliott Trudeau, "The Asbestos Strike," edited by Pierre Elliott Trudeau, translated by James Boake, James Lewis and Samuel, Toronto, 1974.
6. Gazette, Montreal, July 26, 1977.
7. Robert Rumilly, "L'Infiltration Gauchiste au Canada Francais," Ottawa, 1956. All of Rumilly's subsequent quotes in this chapter are from this book.

8

"Democracy First!"

Perhaps partially as a result of Rumilly's attack, some members of Le Rassemblement were quite sensitive about the movement being identified with the socialist CCF or its Quebec wing, the Parti Social Démocratique.

These feelings erupted at a special congress of the movement held over the weekend of March 30 and 31, 1957, and divided the members. By then, the movement claimed 511 members in five sections, spread among 38 towns and cities in Quebec.

There was a group of hardliners who wanted a "closed door" policy against anyone who was a member and active supporter of any political party, even if he belonged to a party whose goals and structures were recognized by Le Rassemblement as democratic.

But there were immediate objections. Why should a member of Le Rassemblement be prevented from supporting a democratic party? That was hardly democratic itself.

Then there was the "open door" group, who were prepared to admit anyone who subscribed to the principles, goals and constitution of the movement. But again people objected, saying Le Rassemblement would expose itself to infiltration by undemocratic elements and could be swamped.

The debate raged for four hours and finally a compromise was struck. A motion was passed allowing anyone to become a member who believed in the constitution, goals and principles of Le Rassemblement provided that he didn't belong to or actively support an association whose goals or means of action were incompatible.

More precisely, the motion specified the following would be excluded: any group advocating discrimination on the basis of colour, race or religion; any totalitarian group, notably those of communist and fascist origins and anyone who was an organizer, official or active supporter of the Liberal, Conservative or National Union parties.

While the movement said it didn't want to openly identify with the Parti Social Démocratique, it had to be recognized that it was the only truly democratic party in Quebec. But some still insisted that to allow senior officials of that party to become members would identify it, in the public's eyes, with the PSD.

To that, someone noted that the two movements weren't incompatible, and that a person could be an active supporter of both. Again, there was a compromise solution, which allowed PSD members to join Le Rassemblement, but they could be expelled if they identified the movement with their party through any declarations or other action.

Le Rassemblement's actions were winning it recognition outside the boundaries of Quebec. About three weeks after the congress a left-wing academic, Michael Oliver, spoke of the movement to the Manitoba Educational Association. According to a later report, Oliver, who was the chairman of the department of political science at United College in Winnipeg, said Quebec was "seeing the development of a body of left-wing opinion which will affect the Church and the nationalist movement in the province".

That development "may have a profound effect on Canadian politics". Three recent events in Quebec had been significant: the publication of The Asbestos Strike, "which challenged the whole social and economic basis of the province and the nationalist ideology which has dominated Quebec's past"; the book on provincial political immorality by Dion and O'Neill and the establishment of Le Rassemblement.

The latter movement had a "left-wing, social democratic flavour" and even if it failed, predicted Oliver, "I do not think the current thought will die in Quebec".[1]

That kind of assessment of Le Rassemblement was just the thing to enrage Rumilly. In May he wrote another small book, along the lines of his first one, and called it "The Tactics of the Left Unmasked".

In it he claimed his first book on the "Leftist Infiltration of French Canada" was vindicated by subsequent events and responded to critics of it.

The reactions by leftists to his first book, as Rumilly later admitted, were "torrents of insults" and "an explosion of hate".

The reason for the hate and the insults, said Rumilly, was that he had exposed the leftists' "clandestine infiltration" of unions, universities and nationalist societies.

"They weren't acting in broad daylight," wrote Rumilly, "because they knew that left-wing ideas were repugnant to the French Canadian people."

Reaction to "Leftist Infiltration" was so strong it became known as the Rumilly Affair in the press. In "Tactics of the Left Unmasked", Rumilly noted that Le Devoir had taken about two months to respond to his first book and then did so flippantly.

An article had appeared February 16, 1957, signed "LEX," which Rumilly said was the nom de plume of Jacques Perrault, the president of the newspaper.

LEX had thanked Rumilly for the gratuitous publicity Le Devoir had received and said the least he could do was to return the favour by suggesting more material for another book.

When Le Rassemblement had held a meeting in early April, 1957, in Montreal, Rumilly observed with satisfaction that the movement stated that it identified with the socialist party, even though there were some objections by Ottawa delegates.

Some delegates complained that membership in the movement was refused to those who weren't members of the CCF, then Canada's socialist party.

Jean Marchand, secretary-general of the Catholic Labour Confederation of Canada said there was a marked tendency in Le Rassemblement toward the socialist party and suggested that if the two were so similar perhaps Le Rassemblement ought to simply join the CCF.

Robert Ouellette, a former socialist candidate [for whom Trudeau had campaigned] added:

"The principles of Le Rassemblement and the Social Democratic Party are so identical that there's no problem belonging to both at the same time."

Rumilly then quoted the article on the speech by Michael Oliver entitled "Left-Wing Opinion Growing Quebec Force."

Rumilly devoted much of his second book to reiterating his theory of the strong link between the French and French Canadian Catholics of the Left. Where did it all start? Rumilly recalled the special Esprit edition written by Cité Libristes.

"It was this edition which really launched left-wing thought in French Canada," concluded Rumilly.

In the months following Le Rassemblement's special congress, two suicides of public figures shook English and French Canada. On April 4, Herbert Norman, the Canadian ambassador to Egypt, leapt from the ninth-floor rooftop of a Cairo apartment building. He had been linked in an American investigation with a communist spy ring, and evidence later surfaced that he had, in the past, been a member of a communist study group.

The following month Jacques Perrault, the publisher of Le Devoir, had committed suicide. Perrault's last major achievement had been in the field of civil liberties, when he successfully had the Supreme Court of Canada overturn the Padlock Law, which Duplessis had passed 30 years before to seize communist propaganda.

During that winter and spring, Trudeau's friend at the University of Montreal, Pierre Dansereau, had been busy planning and organizing an overseas trip for Canadian students by the World University Service.

The students were to visit Ghana June 17 to July 7, 1957, only three months after it had become independent under its first president, the charismatic, Marxist Kwame Nkrumah.

Dansereau decided to invite Trudeau to come on the trip to lend some life to the activities.

Jane Banfield, one of the organizers with Dansereau, recalled that since Trudeau had "paid his own way, . . . he was under no obligation and he just wandered around on his own. He was very seductive to a number of French Canadian students who would attach themselves to him. He was a bit like a Pied Piper, he just led them along."

The group of students from across Canada assembled in New York May 24 and visited the United Nations before flying to London three days later. There, they stayed for a few days again, visiting the House of Commons and other places before flying to Lagos, Nigeria for a three day stopover. After a short time, the group split into different study tours, and Trudeau accompanied one travelling to Benin and eastern Nigeria—later known as Biafra. Two of the students with him were Robert Kaplan and Tim Porteous.

They arrived in Benin June 11 and visited a tribal chief. Porteous recalls learning, in a peculiar way, a shocking bit of news. "We'd gone to see the Oba of Benin in his African palace with all his wives. There was a radio loudspeaker over his head and the news came over about Diefenbaker being elected!"

After their side trips the students again assembled in Ibadan, this time for a marathon bus trip through Dahomey and Togo to Accra, Ghana, starting 4 a.m. Sunday.

The prospect wasn't appealing. Moreover, no provision had been made to visit any French African states for the French Canadian students on the trip. Trudeau had a solution, and asked a small group "O.K. Which of you have your passports?" Trudeau, Porteous and two French Canadian girls made a party of four.

"We decided to strike off on our own on a mammy wagon," recalls Porteous. "They're trucks owned by women and you pay so many cents a mile. They carried goats and chickens and Europeans just didn't travel on them."

In the colonial pecking order of those days, it was a memorable privilege for a "bush" African to sit beside and converse with a European.

The four made their way to Cotonou, Dahomey and checked in at the Hotel de la Plage. "The atmosphere was hedonistic. We had an agreeable weekend," Porteous said without expanding. On Saturday they met a French official and decided to visit a nearby lake village built on stilts over the water.

They hopped in a leaky dugout canoe and started paddling to the village, the boatman bailing all the while. In the middle of the lake, he asked for more money.

"When the French official baulked, he stopped bailing . . . some satisfactory solution was soon arrived at." They finally reached the village and "met little black children speaking the most articulate French".

They had arranged to meet the students' bus in Cotonou, and Porteous remembers vividly its arrival.

"We had a leisurely lunch with wine and climbed on board the bus, filled with half-dead students. They had been going since 4 a.m. and were exhausted, hot and dusty."

Porteous had had a row with Dansereau over whether he could accompany Trudeau on the private trip. Dansereau says "there were times when Trudeau's infringement on discipline was a real thorn in my side". In Porteous' view, "Trudeau didn't have to follow the structures and he provided an element of anarchy".

The bus finally arrived at Accra, where the students moved into quarters at University College in time to begin a series of seminars June 17.

Lewis Perinbam, another organizer of the trip, recalls Trudeau's attitude.

"Conforming to the discipline of the seminars was totally against his nature—so he did his own thing."

"His own thing" clearly irritated other Canadian professors on the trip. Grant Davy, an associate professor of political science at the University of Alberta recalled: "He gave me the impression at that time of being a gadfly, both intellectually and in the sense of flitting about to various parts of the countries we visited. He had a tendency to involve himself only to the point of stirring things up and then to disappear, leaving the consequences of his interventions to those of us who had to deal with the unexciting but necessary routine of baby-sitting some 40 unruly students. I recall rather vaguely several conversations I had with other staff members on our seminar about Trudeau— those who knew him (or at least knew his reputation) confirmed that he had a penchant for stirring things up and then running from the consequences."[2]

115

Leonard Thompson, a professor of history at the University of Cape Town in South Africa, had a similarly unfavourable picture of him.

"The impression I have is that at that stage Mr. Trudeau had the outward style of a hippy and that he was usually seen alone, and with a banjo or similar musical instrument."

Trudeau participated both with Thompson and Davy in a panel discussion on Canadian federalism, but the details are lost. Porteous only recalls Trudeau "setting out with a great deal of clarity and precision his position on federalism".

With that discussion and a short, final burst of activity, the tour wound down and the student group left for London for an evaluation session and two weeks of free time.

Trudeau, back in Canada, began preparing for another trip, this one more perilous and within Canada.

He and Frank Scott of McGill University spent three weeks drifting down the Mackenzie River in the Northwest Territories. They took in the first meeting of the fledgling Northwest Territories Council and Trudeau found time to work on a long essay that would finally launch him in English Canadian academic circles.

Then it was back to Quebec, where he attended an annual conference of the Institut Canadien des Affaires Publiques from September 25 to 29 at Ste. Adèle. The theme of the conference was "Canada and The World Community" and the French influence was notable as it had been the year before.

In the 1956 meeting, Henri-Irenée Marrou, of Esprit fame, had been invited to speak, and the next year an invitation was extended to Raymond Aron, a French philosopher.

One of those who gave a presentation at the 1957 meeting was Jules Leger, who was later to become governor general of Canada. In viewing the international scene, he deplored the constant threat of nuclear incineration and the wide economic inequality between western and "third world" countries. He also strongly criticized the Soviets.

"Russia has a right to life: she has a right to respect. But the place of the Red Army is not in foreign territory where its presence isn't allowed anymore . . . That Tunisia, Indonesia and Malaysia are becoming independent states, all right. But that Hungary and other satellite states continue to be chained to Moscow, no. One of the most outrageous duplicities in contemporary history is the support that the U.S.S.R. gives to revolutionary movements in colonial territories on one hand, and its political intransigence toward its own satellite countries on the other."

Trudeau directed his thoughts and discourse in a different direction, toward the United States and economic domination.

"Political domination and economic domination are inextricably mixed. That was demonstrated only a few years ago by two American ambassadors in Guatemala who became mercenaries for United Fruit.

"In the key sectors of the Canadian economy, non-residents are in the position to take decisions contrary to the welfare of Canadians.

"This leads us to the following question: Can Canada free itself from the domination that the foreigner, and especially the American, exercises on its economy?" It couldn't free itself from domination the same way the Americans freed themselves from theirs. The British had given them long term loans which they repaid, but the Americans had invested money in Canada, and now owned much of its economy.

"American capital could just be excluded, but that would be reactionary and result in a rapid decrease in our economic expansion and radically reduce our standard of living. There are two other possibilities. We could passively submit to American domination . . . or we could vigorously intervene in the play of economic forces.

"Labour unions must be encouraged to obtain for our workers maximum salaries, leaving minimum profits to the foreigner.

"As far as an obligation on Canadian companies dominated by American capital to sell common shares to Canadians is concerned, this policy would only make sense if: Canadians are ready to save more or disinvest from less profitable sectors and the government is ready – unless the private sector is – to acquire for itself these shares, which would mean partial nationalization of the company.

"In conclusion, you can see that a country under the thumb of economic domination can only get out from under it if it practices planning. For that, Canadian nationalism would have to become economically interventionist, and politicians would have to think more about the common good than their election warchest.

"But that's probably asking too much. Canadians want an economic regime that has all the advantages of being controlled; but they want to get them without a controlled economy . . . "[3]

Three weeks after Trudeau's 38th birthday, the annual meeting of Le Rassemblement was called for the weekend of December 10, 1957 in Quebec City.

After a long discussion, delegates decided to change the orientation of the movement slightly. They would put more emphasis on research and study and less on action and expansion.

"Political parties can sleep soundly!" read a report on the meeting of Jacque Hébert's newspaper, Vrai. "It's not during this year that any political action by Le Rassemblement is going to bother them."[4]

Trudeau and Dansereau stepped down as vice-president and president, and were replaced by Jean Phillippe of Montreal and René Tremblay, a professor of social science at Laval University.

Trudeau still remained on the executive, however, with Hébert, Jean-Paul Lefebvre, Pelletier and Guy Hamel.

Three commissions were formed during the meeting to study education, the electoral map and civil liberties.

For Trudeau, the next year was similar to 1956, in that it marked his involvement in a new political movement and was notable for his writings.

His friend, Jacques Hébert, had asked him "to write something or other about democracy" for his readers and Trudeau went to work. The result was far from what Hébert had been banking on. He had thought he would receive one article, perhaps feature-length, but instead Trudeau submitted a 20-part series that was serialized from February 15 to July 15.

"He would write out his articles by hand, taking great pains, proceeding with great caution," recalls Hébert. Sometimes, even when the type was being set for the weekly edition, Trudeau would rush in saying "I know it may be too late—but could I change this comma?"

Trudeau opened the series by quoting Plato: "The heaviest penalty for declining to engage in politics is to be ruled by someone inferior to yourself."

The series was unlike most of Trudeau's other writings, in that it was part argument, part chronicle and part philosophy.

"We give politicians the power of life and death over us; we authorize them to send us to war, imprison us, tax us, regulate our activity, expropriate our houses, discipline our children, supervise our conduct, our reading and our speech . . .

"And we absent-mindedly bestow these absolute powers over our lives and welfare on a handful of men, in elections dominated by fanaticism and gangsterism, generally without asking them the smallest guarantee of intelligence or of elementary honesty.

"We are going to be governed whether we like it or not . . . we must therefore concern ourselves with politics, as Pascal said, to mitigate, as a far as possible the damage done by the madness of our rulers."

Trudeau examined the nature of authority and concluded, "political authority exists only so far as men want to obey". He then went out on the streets to challenge the authority of the Duplessis government by helping to lead University of Montreal students, with the students of five other Quebec universities, in boycotting classes for a day to protest a fee increase. It was admittedly civil disobedience, but it was justified "as a last resort against illegitimate and tyrannical governments".

The State had to be tamed, to be made a servant of the people. Only then might it be turned to "teaching brigades to develop our minds" or knocking down "slums to protect our way of life . . . I want the State to do more, but only after we have stopped thinking of it as an absolute master".

Some of Trudeau's writings received hostile reactions from conservative elements, which Trudeau had deliberately provoked.

"I was setting a snare for all the watchdogs of reaction. I might have known that I would find Mr. Dagenais in it, on all fours along with Leopold Richer."

There was a taunt apparently delivered to Duplessis: "One can say . . . that a prime minister 'gives himself' to his country or province, in the sense that the time he devotes to the administration of public business is out of proportion to the indemnity he receives from the public treasury.

"But it does not necessarily follow that such a gift is always to the advantage of the recipients: there are some gifts one would do well not to accept, as the Trojans learned to their cost some years ago!"

Three-quarters of the way through his series, Trudeau posed this question: "What regime, or what system, gives the maximum guarantee against oppression?

"A possible reply here would be that it is conceivable that a benevolent despot might rule wisely, establish a just order for all his subjects, and leave them enough freedom of expression. Would such a regime not be based on the consent of the people?

"Yes, this is conceivable. But such consent clearly could not be taken for granted. A mechanism would have to be provided to allow the people to express their opinions freely on the excellence of the despot. There would also have to be some device to ensure that the despot would abdicate if opinion went against him. And finally a means would have to be invented to designate, peacefully, a successor whom the people would agree to obey. But clearly such a regime would no longer be called a despotism; it would have borrowed the actual mechanism of democracy.

"And it must be recognized that democracy is the form of government we are looking for."

He didn't find much of it in Quebec. The National Union government "stands supreme in its contempt for freedom . . . I hold no brief for the Liberal opposition – on the contrary its mediocrity is partly to blame for the ills we suffer. But I choke with indignation at the humiliations inflicted on that opposition.

"The Duplessis government, by buffoonery, contempt, accusation, insult, intimidation, illegality, and fraud, has prevented the parliamentary opposition from performing its functions and has therefore gagged the people in the persons of its best-accredited representatives."[5]

While Trudeau had been writing about democracy and good government, powerful men had taken over major countries, through the ballot box and otherwise.

On March 27, a stubby, partly-bald man with the face of a peasant took over the reins of power in the U.S.S.R., Nikita Khrushchev. In France, on June 1, the wartime leader and general Charles de Gaulle became the president of the Fifth Republic, while closer to home, there was another federal election in Canada. After Diefenbaker had won his minority victory in June, 1957, the Liberals had made Lester Pearson the leader of their party. Diefenbaker's minority was unworkable. He decided to go to the polls March 31, and was rewarded with the largest majority in Canadian history – 208 of 264 seats.

A month later Trudeau observed in Cité Libre that although the election campaign was "very prolific in promises of all sorts, there was nothing offered which could let us hope that the elected government would drag Canada a little way out of its position of an economy heavily dominated by the foreigner".

While the old parties had made much of pan-Canadian nationalism, paradoxically, the Social Democratic Party "hardly blew the trumpets of nationalism at all; but it was the only one to propose a controlled economy, indispensable to the transformation of the above nationalism into economic reality".

Trudeau then repeated almost verbatim his speech to the Institut Canadien des Affaires Publiques of the previous fall to give his readers an idea of what kind of price they would have to pay for economic independence.

He concluded by saying that Canada wouldn't automatically grow out of its economic domination. First, the country had to want its independence. But it was by no means certain that Canadians really wanted that, since politicians had never really exposed them to the alternatives.

"No one really knows, then, if the Canadian people would be prepared to gently slow down the tempo of progress, in case it was necessary, to gain relative economic independence.

121

"Above all, no one knows if Canadians would be ready to accept the sort of economic control that all these reforms suppose. And if one thing is emphasized by the present examination, it's that a country under the thumb of economic domination can't escape to its advantage unless it practises a measure of planning.

"But who talks about that to Canadians aside from the Social Democratic Party? Ironically, the most nationalist parties (federal as much as provincial) are those who most oppose economic intervention. These politicians would like an economic system which would have all the advantages of control; but they will fight to the death against the controlled economy! For moneylenders should always preserve their rights, shouldn't they ... "[6]

Trudeau's thoughts and writings continued to be dominated by democracy and nationalism, the desirability of the first and the reactionary negativism of the second. He examined them in Canada and Quebec in his essay "Some Obstacles To Democracy in Quebec," which appeared in August in the Canadian Journal of Political Science.

Much of it was drawn from previous works: his speech to the founding convention of the Institut Canadien Des Affaires Publiques in the fall of 1954, entitled "Obstacles to Democracy"; his contribution to The Asbestos Strike and "Réflexions Sur la Politique au Canada Francais", a Cité Libre article he had written for the August, 1952 edition.

Perhaps it was just as well for Trudeau that the essay was published in English in a journal outside Quebec because of what he had to say about his fellow French Canadians.

"Historically, French Canadians have not really believed in democracy for themselves ...

"In all important aspects of national politics, guile, compromise, and a subtle kind of blackmail decided their course and determined their alliances. They appeared to discount all political or social ideologies, save nationalism ... "

French Canadians voted "only for the man or group which stood for their ethnic rights ...

"Their civic sense was corrupted and they became political immoralists ... "

Not all the blame was apportioned to the French Canadians. To a large degree, English Canadians (who didn't want democracy for anyone save themselves) and the Church (which rejected democracy as the child of revolution) were to blame.

Also to blame was the Liberal party, both federal and provincial. From 1891 to 1958 Quebec had given the Liberals a majority of their seats, nearly always an overwhelming majority.

It was this party which deserved credit "for preventing the growth in Quebec of a federal nationalist party..."

Liberals "learned to cater to French Canada's intuition that its destinies would be better protected at Ottawa by a more or less independent bloc within the party in power rather than by a nationalist party bound, because of its ethnic basis, to remain forever seated on opposition benches.

"If French Canadians even today have learnt so little about democracy, if they twist its rules so shockingly, if they are constantly tempted by authoritarianism, it is to a large degree because the Liberal Party has been miserably remiss in its simple political duty. Instead of educating the French-speaking electorate to believe in democracy, the Liberals seemed content to cultivate the ignorance and prejudice of that electorate."

Liberals "have always encouraged Quebecers to continue using their voting bloc as an instrument of racial defence, or of personal gain. Their only slogans have been racial slogans... 'Vote for a party led by a French Canadian'... and it was on the strength of such slogans that they were elected.

"The shameful incompetence of the average Liberal M.P. from Quebec was a welcome asset to a Government that needed little more than a herd of performing asses to file in when the division bell rang. The party strategists had but to find an acceptable stablemaster... and the trained donkeys sitting in the back benches could be trusted to behave."

Trudeau wasn't content to merely describe and rail against the obstacles to democracy in Quebec – he wanted them torn down. It was becoming apparent that Le Rassemblement wouldn't be able to do the job, at least not on its own, after it had resolved at its last congress not to actively try to expand its membership, and to concentrate on research rather than action.

He decided to do something himself and his initiative took the form of a 31-page manifesto published in the October, 1958 edition of Cité Libre. It was a call to all democratic forces opposing Duplessis to unite and defeat him, and as such, gave the clearest public view yet of his thoughts on political tactics and strategy.

Quickly reviewing the three opposition parties in Quebec, these are the conclusions he came to. The Liberal Party was compromised because the federal wing had had a "non-aggression pact" with Duplessis for years, while the provincial wing floundered about without a viable alternative to him.

The Social Democratic Party was the only opposition party that was founded on a political ideology and provided answers to social problems based on "a positive political thought, clearly identifiable and generally coherent". But the party carried little weight in the province, and what progress it had made was at a "frightening" cost in time and human energy, which had resulted in a high turnover of activists who were for the most part young and inexperienced.

These elements of youth and high turnover resulted in a certain dogmatism in the party, which was perhaps why it had "obstinately refused any formula for Le Rassemblement which wasn't an exact replica of the SDP's".

But this rigidity and isolationism might be in the process of disappearing. The previous April, the Canadian Labour Congress had passed a resolution which recognized that "the need is felt for a popular political movement with a very large base which will group together the SDP, the union movement, farmers' organizations, members of liberal professions and all others of liberal spirit . . . "

Then the following July, the national congress of the SDP had voted to adhere to the CLC resolution after Stanley Knowles, one of the party's leading personalities, declared "It's now time to build an organization which will be the party of a greater number of citizens".

"The dialectic of action is urgently forcing us to concentrate our effective people on a sole objective: democracy," Trudeau wrote. "Those who refuse to help in the installation of a political democracy, under the pretext that they themselves are preparing for an economic and social democracy, are committing a very serious strategic error. For at all costs, the envelope of democracy must be made before dividing up the contents.

"The seizure of power by Hitler and Mussolini was greatly facilitated by the internal divisions of the anti-fascist forces."

While Duplessis wasn't being compared to the fascist dictators, there was the same element of urgency. "If the same government succeeds in dominating the next legislative assembly without a vigorous opposition, there's a strong bet that what's left of our progressive institutions will be irrevocably damaged or checkmated.

"I believe in the necessity of state control to maximize the liberty and welfare of all, and to permit everyone to realize himself fully. But I would prefer to renounce socialism rather than admit that one should construct it on undemocratic foundations: Russia has shown us that that is the way of totalitarianism. As far as 'national' socialism goes, that holds little attraction for me, either.

"And that's why I'm in no hurry to call for nationalizations and controls in the province of Quebec..." The State was already characterized by "incompetence, fraud and oppression" and would people be better served if its responsibilities were enlarged to owning and controlling hospitals, universities, industry etc.?

"Democracy first, that should be the rallying cry of all the reformist forces in the province." Those who believed in free enterprise should join with those who believed in socialism in achieving democracy.

"As far as I go, it seems evident to me that the regime of free enterprise has shown itself incapable of adequately resolving problems posed in education, health, housing, full employment etc. That's why I'm personally convinced that with the upheavals promised by automation, cybernetics and thermo-nuclear energy, liberal democracy will not long be able to satisfy our growing demands for justice and liberty, and that it should evolve toward a form of social democracy. But I am willing to help with the establishment of a liberal democracy precisely because I believe the other will follow afterwards. A liberal democrat will doubtless be convinced otherwise; but what does that matter?

"The conclusion is clear. Let's regroup free men about a common objective, democracy . . . To attain this objective and propagate this ideology . . . let's move toward the formation of a new movement: the democratic union.

"Historically, many liberal democracies, as in England and Sweden, have evolved toward socialism.

"Parliamentary democracy such as we know it is a game for two: if there are more than two parties present, the government . . . is strong from the division of the opposition parties. Consequently, to prevent governmental tyranny, these should fuse together . . . In other terms, third parties are only valuable if they can effect a breakthrough and destroy the second party. And, this breakthrough hasn't succeeded on the national level, and even more so, will not succeed in our province."

The democratic union was an umbrella group for all democrats to gather under. "For example, Jean-Louis Gagnon, Gerard Picard and Jacques Hébert have about the same ideas on social democracy; but the first is a militant Liberal, the second is of SDP persuasion and the third edits the newspaper of the Civic Action League. Historically speaking, one can't expect Gagnon to enter the SDP or the others to make similar conversions. But one ought to be able to expect them to collaborate in common action in a new democratic formation.

"Existing parties would be able to preserve their own identities while forming, for a definite period, a common front in the double goals of defeating the regime and accomplishing a minimum program of action."

In the time remaining before the next election, a watch committee should be set up so that democratic forces would not be caught off their guard.

"The committee would be able to sign and publish a document asking the leaders of the various groups to make known their opinions on the present plans for a rapprochement."

126

FOOTNOTES CHAPTER 8

1. Gazette, April 25, 1957.

2. From a letter to the author. Davy, who the next year became the leader of the Liberal Party Federation in Alberta, qualified his comments, however. He went on to say, "I should hasten to add, lest my above comments lead to the wrong conclusion, that I have come to have considerable respect for Mr. Trudeau since 1972 and to re-assess my superficial impressions of his intellect gained in such a short time in Ghana."

3. From the "Rapport de la Quatrième Conférence Annuelle de L'Institut Canadien des Affaires Publiques".

4. Vrai, December 14, 1957.

5. Quotes from this series are taken in translation from Pierre Elliott Trudeau, "Approaches to Politics," translated by I. M. Owen, the Oxford University Press, Toronto, 1970.

6. Pierre Elliott Trudeau, "À Propos de Domination Économique," Cité Libre, May, 1958.

9

Cuba and China

Events were moving quickly in the fall of 1958. The CCF and the Canadian Labour Congress were talking about a new party, similar to the Labour Party of Britain, and the Quebec Federation of Labour was lending its support to the idea as well.

The national Liberal Party under Lester Pearson was evidently frightened at the prospect of seeing much of its electoral base taken over by the new party.

William Dodge, the administrative vice-president of the CLC, was invited to the congress of the party's executive committee in Edmonton and heard Pearson declare that Liberals should position themselves ideologically "left of centre".[1] That didn't impress Dodge, who said he believed the Liberals were more interested in votes than elaborating a political ideology.

To make matters worse for the Liberals, Jean Lesage, their Quebec chief and former federal cabinet minister, said "liberalism is neither to the left, nor to the right, it's in the centre".

An annual meeting of Le Rassemblement was called for Saturday, November 29, and a few days beforehand press reports indicated that the movement was considering the move by the CCF, CLC and Quebec Federation of Labour to form a new party.

Trudeau was then elected president of Le Rassemblement, replacing René Tremblay who stood down.

He had said in his Democratic Manifesto that Le Rassemblement could take the lead in bringing about a rapprochement of democratic forces, and now he was in a good position to help it happen. Backing him up were Jacques Hébert, Francine Laurendeau (the daughter of André and former head of the CCF Youth), Gerard Pelletier, Jean Marchand and Jean-Paul Lefebvre, all on the executive, and Micheline Legendre as treasurer.

So far, all had gone according to Trudeau's plan as laid out in his manifesto. The next step was the creation of a watch committee made up of leading personalities from different sectors of society and the issuing of their own manifesto.

That took about four months to put together, but on Friday, April 10, 1959, the committee had been formed and held its first press conference.

It made front page news in Le Devoir under the heading "21 Personalities Launch an Urgent Call to Opposition Parties: Let's Unite!" The personalities on the committee, an impressive list, came from the Liberal and Social Democratic Parties, the Quebec Federation of Labour, the Civic Action League, the Catholic Labour Confederation of Canada, universities and of course, Le Rassemblement.

The names included: Jean-Charles Falardeau, Trudeau, Pelletier, Marchand, Marc Brière, Jean-Paul Geoffroy, Jacques Hébert, Hector Langevin, Micheline Legendre and Jean-Robert Ouellette.

The committee made public a manifesto "exhorting the leaders of the political parties to 'openly indicate their adherence' in principle to an agreement which would result in one of the three following plans: a) the fusion of different groups and the creation of a new party; b) an alliance based on a minimum program with each party preserving its identity; c) the formation of an electoral front ensuring the presence in each riding of a sole opposition candidate."[2]

During the course of the press conference the committee's 21 members made it clear they weren't representing their parties or organizations. "On the contrary," explained Trudeau, "for now anyway, it's concerned with favouring the regrouping of opposition forces by agitating within the limits of each formation."

Brière, a Liberal who worked on the party's newspaper, La Réforme, noted that the provincial wing of the Liberal Party at its last congress in Ottawa in December struck a committee "to study the eventual regrouping of opposition forces".

Jean-Robert Ouellette of the SDP said his party also had a similar committee and the idea of a regrouping of forces was welcome there.

Pelletier said workers weren't having any problems wrestling with "party loyalty", as the only loyalty they had was to democratic objectives.

As Pierre Laporte, the political columnist of Le Devoir noted a short time afterward, the manifesto aroused much interest among the different parties and movements, but they were being cagey and cautious about committing themselves.

The Liberals found the manifesto's proposals "not impossible", the Civic Action League thought they were "premature" and the SDP said that before they committed themselves to any political action there would have to be some agreement on ideas and political principles.[3]

Those who signed the manifesto went back to their respective organizations and parties to start delicate negotiations.

About a month after the declaration of the "21" Trudeau's friend at Le Devoir, Jean-Marc Léger, interviewed him as one of a series of French Canadian personalities on "Where is French Canada Going?"

It was an extraordinary interview, headed "To restore liberty and justice, let's do away with the alliance between the champions and profiteers of the status quo".

"I dream of a people whose heart and spirit are open to the world," Léger quoted Trudeau as saying.

"The major problem is that there is a truly damnable pact between those who want to maintain the spiritual and intellectual status quo and those who want to maintain the political and economic status quo . . .

"There are, for example, some nationalists and members of the clergy who would joyfully look upon transformations in our economic and political structures; but in the final account, they condemn the activities of those who get mixed up with it because—having thought about it—they seemed to inevitably involve modifications to the sacred and ethnocentric nature of our society."

Some of the members of a group who had signed a "blood pact" to support the status quo were the Abbé Desrosiers of Nos Cours, Pat Walsh, Robert Rumilly and Father Ledit. He then looked at the touchy topics of provincial autonomy and nationalism.

"In the present context this battle [for autonomy] only makes sense if it's concerned with the autonomy of the human being. The rest is just a joke....

"What's necessary in our province in concrete terms is to help the poor, tear down the slums, put the people into schools, open doors to culture, chase uneducated minds out of our universities and the bandits from politics... once this revolution is accomplished, if there are still people who speak French and go to church, great, so much the better for those who will later want to call the operation nationalist...

"I see only one essential rule—pragmatism; only one spirit—audacity and only one technique—agitation...

"In one stroke we could lessen our demographic inferiority, find the solution to our educational crisis and remedy our mediocrity in linguistic matters, by systematically favouring the immigration to Canada of primary school teachers from France."

In the weeks following this interview, negotiations with various groups and parties to form the democratic union proceeded apace.

It was during this hiatus that Robert Rumilly struck again, with a third book in his series about leftist infiltration in French Canada, called "Socialists Dominate the Leftist Network". His timing was either a result of fast work, or uncanny luck.

While he didn't go into the attempts to form the democratic union, he reviewed events since his last book, "The Tactics of the Leftists Unmasked", in the spring of 1957.

He had written previously that Le Devoir was part of the "leftist network" in Quebec, but now, he said, La Presse, the province's largest French language daily, had joined it.

The newspaper's editor, Roger Mathieu, had been elected

president of the Catholic Labour Confederation of Canada, and asked for a leave of absence from La Presse with a guarantee he could return to his post afterwards.

The paper's management agreed to the leave, but refused to guarantee his post, and a strike broke out October 2, 1958. The owners of the paper appointed Antoine Geoffrion, a member of the administrative council of La Presse, to settle the strike.

But Geoffrion was also the treasurer of the Liberal Party and a good friend of Jean-Louis Gagnon, one of the party's most left-wing members and editor of its paper, La Réforme.

The result was that Gagnon was made editor of La Presse and the strike was finally settled. Under his influence, the newspaper soon showed a new inclination, said Rumilly.

"La Presse gave considerable importance, and great publicity, to a manifesto of Pierre Elliott Trudeau and to a public meeting of Le Rassemblement [where Trudeau was also the prime mover], while being careful not to indicate that the meeting only brought together 35 people, some of whom were merely curious bystanders or opponents."

The Canadian Broadcasting Corporation's French service, Radio-Canada, had swung even farther to the left. The most frequent contributors to its "cultural" affairs programs were Pelletier, André Laurendeau, Gagnon, Trudeau and Lévesque, representing the same old groups: Le Devoir, Vrai, Cité Libre, Le Rassemblement, L'Institut Canadien des Affaires Publiques and the Social Democratic Party.

Gagnon had arranged to have his younger brother, Claude, placed in Radio-Canada where he administered the budget of the cultural affairs programs. Mrs. Jeanne Sauvé, a producer, was the wife of Maurice Sauvé, the newly appointed head of the provincial Liberal Party and director of the L'Institut Canadien. Roger Rolland, of Cité Libre, was the general director of programming, and his cohorts at the review such as Reginald Boisvert, Guy Cormier and Gilles Marcotte, were involved in one way or another with Radio-Canada.

Rumilly further listed another 17 persons in Radio-Canada, many related to each other by blood or marriage, who were closely tied in with "the great liberal-socialist family".

The work this network had set itself was clear.

"Take Pierre Elliott Trudeau, for example. Here's quite an ordinary guy, a very average man, who only has a certain personal fortune. No one would dare to attribute to him what's called talent. Without Radio-Canada none outside the little Cité Libre circle would have heard of him. Radio-Canada took him, made him, interviewed him on all sorts of topics, lavished all sorts of opportunities on him and to a certain extent fashioned him. It put him on the map, as the saying goes. The name of Pierre Elliott Trudeau was projected, acclaimed, repeated hundreds of times to hundreds of thousands of listeners. It's thus that Pierre Elliott Trudeau can pass for an important personage today. His initiatives and interventions carry some weight. All of it, in the service of socialist ideas. Hundreds of young people much more gifted than Pierre Elliott Trudeau didn't have the same chance because they weren't on the left."

A cynical device Radio-Canada used to give the appearance of impartiality was to invite a right-winger onto a program, faced by three or four left-wingers.

As an example, Rumilly cited a program entitled "Do Provincial Rights Protect French Culture?" The producer was Professor Frank Scott of McGill University and two of the guests were the "inevitable ultra-leftist" Pierre Elliott Trudeau and a "left-wing centralizer" from New Brunswick, Gerard Picard. The sole man left to defend provincial autonomy and the right was Noel Dorion, the third guest.

The left was entrenched in the universities as well, both among the academics and the students. Charles Lussier, a Cité Libriste, had married the daughter of Léon Lortie, a "virulent leftist". Lortie was the head of extension studies at the University of Montreal. The student council invited Gagnon, Trudeau, Pelletier, Michel Chartrand and Lévesque to discuss "various problems of education" in March, 1958.

At Laval University in Quebec City, the student council invited Chartrand, chief of the Social Democratic Party in Quebec to speak and printed a detailed report of Trudeau's manifesto for a democratic union in its newspaper. The same issue asked the Church to revise its attitude in the face of "a new political structure, namely Canadian socialism". The next issue gave a detailed account of the congress of the SDP Youth, whose president was a former contributor to the newspaper.

After starting off as an anti-corruption movement in Montreal, the Civic Action League had been infiltrated as well.

The communist front organization, the World Peace Council, held a conference in Stockholm from July 16 to 22, 1958. Who made up the delegation from Quebec? Léon Patenaude, the league's secretary-general, Jacques Hébert, editor of the league's organ, Vrai, and Jean-Pierre Goyer, who had actively campaigned for the league. Goyer was also one of the three students who had participated in a three-month sit-in at Duplessis' office as part of a general student strike in March, 1958. [The other two were Bruno Méloche and Francine Laurendeau, both of whom were among the "21" who had signed the watch committees's manifesto for a democratic union.]

"The 'three delegates from the province of Quebec' are then, in fact, the delegates of the Civic Action League. Nothing more and nothing less."

Communists and "progressives" weren't children – when they invited foreigners to their palavers they wanted sympathizers. Gerard Filion, Hébert and Trudeau, of Le Devoir, Vrai and Cité Libre, had been invited to tour communist China, Poland and Moscow.

"Evidently, only those whom one hopes will render a service are invited. I'm not saying that the principal contributors of Le Devoir and Vrai are communists. The Soviets don't need avowed communists to do their work or spread their propaganda in the province of Quebec.

"What the Soviets need are people with a non-communist appearance, even anti-communist, who occasionally criticize the Soviets on details but who serve their propaganda on points judged essential."

Trudeau and others had also been active with left-wing members of the church. Georges-Henri Lévesque, "a distinguished Dominican," had transformed the faculty of social sciences at Laval University, where he was dean, into "a leftist cell, and naturally, centralizing". He also transformed a Dominican retreat house, Maison Montmorency, into "a political club, of liberal-socialist tendencies".

For instance, in January, 1958, there was a four-day seminar on political immorality in Quebec. Among the principal participants were Abbés Louis O'Neill and Gerard Dion, Michel Chartrand, Trudeau and a past Liberal candidate, Paul Gérin-Lajoie.

The "handful of men" at the centre of the network were Gagon, Réne Lévesque and Trudeau. "From all sides, French Canadians are receiving directives from these wise men.

"Pierre Elliott Trudeau, one of the principal doctrinaires of the leftist movement, has for a long time thrown French Canadian patriotism to the nettles. Certain of his articles in Cité Libre show a double tendency, Marxist and anti-French Canadian."

The same tendencies came across during the interview Trudeau gave to Jean-Marc Léger.

"Everything must be sundered and revolutionized. While neither troubling oneself with the religious or national aspects," wrote Rumilly of Trudeau.

He quoted Trudeau as saying:

"Once this revolution is accomplished, if there are still people who speak French and go to church, great, so much the better for those who will later want to call the operation nationalist."

Rumilly continued. "To facilitate the upheaval, Pierre Elliott Trudeau advocates 'a systematic immigration of French primary school teachers to Canada'. Neither Pierre Elliott Trudeau nor Jean-Marc Léger, who know the French scene well, can ignore the fact that the overwhelming majority of the primary school teachers of that country are communist. Neither Pierre Elliott Trudeau nor Jean-Marc Léger can ignore the role of these teachers, who are truly priests of a counter-church in the anti-religious struggle in France."

During the summer of 1959 Trudeau went back to Europe and by August found himself in Bonn, buying equipment for the amusement rides at Belmont Park, which his family partially owned.

Micheline Legendre, the secretary-treasurer of Le Rassemblement, met him there and they took a trip along the Rhine Valley in Trudeau's rented Renault. Legendre had first sought his advice in 1954 over whether she should take a cultural trip to Russia. Five years later, she was eager to see communist China, but didn't know how it could be arranged.

She wanted Trudeau to go with her to Japan to try to obtain a visa to visit the country, but he told her, "No, wait until it's a sure thing".

Back in Canada, time won a battle which had so far defeated Trudeau and all his friends and associates.

On September 3, in the town of Shefferville in northern Quebec, Maurice Duplessis died.

It quickly became apparent the National Union was a one-man party as panic and uncertainty spread among the faithful. Paul Sauvé was soon sworn in as premier, but burnt himself out trying to rally the party and died on January 2, 1960.

There was an air of expectancy, a feeling that after 16 consecutive years of rule by the National Union under Duplessis, times were really changing.

It was perhaps the decisive turning point in the struggle which became known as the Quiet Revolution. To the south, exactly one year before Sauvé's death, there had been another revolution, though not so quiet, led by Fidel Castro.

In Quebec the Liberal Party under Jean Lesage was mobilizing for the election. He had recruited René Lévesque as a candidate, a household name through his CBC television program Point de Mire and the strike against the corporation he had led in 1958. Also on Lesage's team was Paul Gérin-Lajoie, a constitutional expert and Rhodes scholar.

While there was strength in the diversity of Lesage's followers, there was also weakness.

Among the loose socialist-liberal coalition in the province and in the Liberal Party a crack had appeared over the old issue, nationalism. The crack would run so deep it would eventually split up close friends and associates, such as the Cité Libre team.

Trudeau, meanwhile, had passed gracefully into middle age.

In October, 1959, he turned 40. He was becoming active in another cause, a group called the Committee for the Control of Radiation Hazards, which had been founded that year with the active assistance of his friend, Pierre Dansereau of the University of Montreal.

He was also working to revamp the administrative structure of Cité Libre. He had asked the advice of his friend, Jacques Hébert, who had suggested expanding it and making it a monthly instead of a quarterly. To finance it, they borrowed an idea from Victor Barbeau of Liaison magazine, and formed a co-operative.

The two quickly found 50 people who invested $100 each to become members and their first issue, in a new format, came out in January, 1960, ten years after the review's inception.

Gerard Pelletier was the director of the editorial committee, with Trudeau and Jean-Charles Falardeau as his assistants. Hébert acted as the "editorial secretary". As well, the three were directors of the provisional administrative council under the presidency of Jean Dostaler. There was also a "supervisory committee" to overlook everyone's activities consisting of Léon Patenaude, of the Civic Action League, Jean Marchand and Jeanne Lapointe.

During the first few months of 1960 Trudeau watched political developments closely. In April, however, he took time off for a little adventure.

He had met Alphonse Gagnon during some labour negotiations. Gagnon was a rich physical fitness enthusiast from Chicoutimi, Quebec, who specialized in ocean canoeing.

Gagnon's ambition was to cross the Florida Straits to Cuba in a canoe rigged with oars that could be operated by foot power. He had already completed a trip down the coast of Florida and had been preparing for the more ambitious venture for more than a year.

Gagnon had written to the American coast guard for details on the straits – currents, winds etc. – and received a warning: "It is a dangerous undertaking and you are strongly advised not to make the attempt."

Not to be intimidated, he put together an 80-page package of documents on the proposed crossing and showed it to Trudeau, who he knew was an avid canoeist. "Want to come?" he asked.

Trudeau, without glancing at the package, replied that if after reading all the information Gagnon was willing to go, so was he.

Neither of them was unprepared for the demanding trip. Both were in good shape, and Gagnon passed on much of his knowledge of the sea to Trudeau.

Part of this knowledge had been gained the hard way when they were skin diving off the Florida coast the year before. Gagnon told him that sharks "will come straight for you and then, six feet away, they'll turn away, so just relax". A shark later approached, Trudeau obediently "just relaxed", and it turned away.

Late April was one of the quietest times of the year to cross the straits, so at 5 a.m. on April 20, 1960, Trudeau, Gagnon and one of his employees, Vilmor Francoeur, left Montreal for Florida.

They arranged for their Cuban visas through the female consul in Key West, whom Gagnon described as "of a certain age, quite disagreeable and stupid. We charitably assumed she was a leftover from the old regime."[4]

If the woman was disagreeable, it may have been because she was unsure of her own position at the time. In Cuba, tension was high, and according to American academic Theodore Draper, Castro was coldly purging his July 26 Movement of non-communists. There had actually been two civil wars under Castro, according to Draper.

"In the first, he had represented a democratic cause, and it had required a civil war against Batista's dictatorship. In the second, he represented a totalitarian alliance with the communists, and it required a civil war against the democratic elements in his own movement."[5]

A stream of refugees fleeing to the U.S. had at first been made up of Batista followers, but later many former Castro followers joined them.

At 12.01 a.m. April 30, Gagnon, Trudeau and Francoeur set

out for Cuba, accompanied by a shrimper that Gagnon had hired.

They made good time that night, but with dawn the wind began to freshen. Three Canadian reporters and photographers aboard the boat to cover the attempt were vomitting regularly despite the dramamine tablets they had swallowed.

The three kept rowing through the day but by 7 p.m., after covering 50 miles in 19 hours of rowing, the winds had reached 40 miles per hour and the attempt had to be abandoned. They boarded the boat and within minutes also became violently ill from the pitching and rolling. They were later told the force eight winds they had endured in their flimsy craft had sunk another shrimper.

Trudeau made his way back to Montreal where the provincial election campaign was about to begin in earnest. But before turning his attentions there, he decided to assess Diefenbaker's accomplishments and policies over the past three years.

It was too soon, Trudeau thought, to pass judgment on the government's policies as a whole as they were just getting used to the reins of power after a generation without them, but not too soon to judge Diefenbaker.

He was a prime minister trying to do too much, with too little, too quickly. If he had proceeded cautiously, with slow, reasoned maturity, "perhaps the Conservative chief would have been able to give his party a truly historical dimension".

Instead, his party was becoming known as a "grab bag of loud mouths" that was all talk and little action. Diefenbaker had tried initiatives in foreign affairs, defence and international trade, but they had all come to nought.

"I really find that a pity. For personally, I was one of those who were convinced that the long King-St. Laurent reign turned the Liberals into an arrogant party short on democratic principles. And since the Conservatives were the only ones to beat them, I consoled myself with the fact that Mr. Diefenbaker seemed to be the man to renew political thought a little ... "[6]

After Sauvé died in January of 1960, Antonio Barrette, the former Quebec minister of labour during the Asbestos Strike, was made premier and began drawing government advisors from the ranks of the opposition outside the legislature.

Trudeau noted that one couldn't be an advisor and opponent at the same time. Barrette's move had the effect of weakening an already weak opposition at a crucial moment.

He feared the much-touted new party, to be formed by the Canadian Congress of Labour and the CCF, would have no Quebec base and would be perceived for the next 25 years as the old CCF had been, as "English" and "foreign".

The Civic Action League and the Social Democratic Party had both refused to throw their support behind the Democratic Union.

"The clear result is that the Liberal Party has obtained at little cost the monopoly of opposition votes. And the corollary is that a René Lévesque—suddenly eager to get involved in the election—finds it a practical impossibility to go anywhere except the Liberals."[7]

But even then, the Liberals might lose or only win by a slim margin.

As it turned out, Trudeau's misgivings were well-founded. There was only a slight percentage swing in the popular vote, giving the Liberals 51 per cent and the National Union 47 per cent. But because the opposition vote hadn't been split by several candidates in each riding, it was enough, and the Liberals took a clear majority of the seats, 50, to the National Union's 44.

Jean-Paul Geoffroy recalls huddling around a television set with Pelletier and Trudeau in Pelletier's home on election night.

"Trudeau said, 'there's only one important aspect of this election: René Lévesque,'" without further explanation.

A month later, after Lévesque had been appointed minister of public works and water resources, he met with Trudeau, Marchand, Pelletier, Jean-Paul Lefebvre and Geoffroy at Trudeau's home. Geoffroy recalled Lévesque asking, "O.K., I'm minister of public works, now I can do something. What do you think I should do? You've got all the ideas."

Trudeau had an answer for his question and gave it publicly. Lévesque's future actions should be guided by the road the provincial Liberal government took in its reform measures.

"If all those who fought Duplessis with the thought, the pen, the word and action don't support the leftist, radical inclinations of the government which they have helped elect . . . it will have to move to the right or die.

"The main reason why the true opposition withheld their loyalty from the Liberals for a decade was that we believed they were incapable of being an effective tool for certain basic reforms and certain structural changes. We emphatically affirm that and the Liberals strongly deny it. And, today, the burst caused by these accumulated denials has propelled the Liberal Party (despite itself?) along a road to reform. And I believe we would be wretched strategists and mediocre citizens if we didn't lend a shoulder to this impetus . . .

"For example, I would be quite surprised if we didn't have to constantly remind the government and those governed what real reforms are in areas like education, natural resources, social legislation, municipal administration and economic orientation.

"In conclusion, I believe that men of action should support the Liberal Party in all its reform undertakings. I believe that they should withdraw this support if it fails in its undertakings and betrays the democratic gamble."[8]

Earlier that summer Trudeau had gone to Micheline Legendre's nearby house in Outremont and suggested she get to work organizing the trip to China that they had talked over the summer before.

Legendre didn't have the faintest idea how to go about it as there was no communist Chinese embassy or consulate in Canada. In desperation, she telephoned Dr. James Endicott in Toronto. He had been publicly identified with communist China since he had sided with the communists in their allegations that Americans had used germ warfare in Korea.

Endicott referred her to Dr. Daniel Longpré, a senior Quebec communist, to arrange the trip. Ironically, it was the same man who had headed a Canadian communist delegation at a meeting in Vienna about eight years earlier, when Trudeau had passed through on his way to Moscow.

Longpré in turn extended a number of invitations to Cité Libre, and allowed them to decide who would go. Madeleine

141

Parent, a trade union organizer in Toronto who had been a communist party member in the past, was also invited. In Montreal, Denis Lazure, who had long been identified with communist front organizations such as the Canadian Peace Congress, of which he had been an executive member, was invited. So were Trudeau, Legendre and Jacques Hébert.

The trip was timed to coincide with China's national day, October 1, and the group left Montreal for London to pick up their visas, arriving there September 13.

Trudeau and Hébert had no illusions about their trip, or the conditions under which it would be taken.

"It is true that . . . we would be largely at the mercy (and it was a mercy) of interpreters; that we would see only what the authorities would let us see; and so on. But the same reservations apply to the testimony of Canadian tourists in Spain, Egypt or the Holy Land . . .

"We know that to some people the mere fact of going to China and staying there at the expense of the Communists is enough to vitiate any testimony. Such people clearly rate their own and others' honesty dirt cheap."

Nor did the prospect of being labelled communists upon their return bother the two very much, "since both of them had been generously reproved, knocked off, and abolished in the integralist and reactionary press in consequence of earlier journeys behind the iron curtain" and "the prospect of being assassinated yet again on their return from China was hardly likely to impress them".

In London Trudeau was almost left behind after the Chinese chargé d'affaires said he wouldn't be issued a visa because he had a Taiwanese entry stamp in his passport. Trudeau readily admitted he had visited Japan, the Phillipines and Taiwan two years earlier, but that didn't signify approval of Chiang Kaishek's regime.

But Trudeau had been elected leader of the group—in his absence—and the others said they would go with him or not at all.

Two days later Trudeau had his visa and all five of them left for Peking via Moscow, Omsk and Irkutsk. Upon their arrival September 18 each was greeted with a bunch of flowers and a total absence of customs or police formalities.

They were put up at the Hotel Hsin Chiao, assigned a Mr. Hou as their constant guide and organizer and given a tour of the city starting the next day.

At a prison they visited they were told prisoners were rehabilitated by "work and education". Trudeau and Hébert drily remarked, "education, in Marxist language, means Marxist education". In workshops "prisoners work in silence while a loudspeaker immerses them in revolutionary sayings and political speeches. They are being re-educated."

There weren't any bolts or locks on cell doors for, "why escape when it has become impossible to hide anywhere in this large country?"

A large commune was next on the itinerary followed by Peking's Institute of Minorities of China, which Trudeau and Hébert found impressive. They met a Tibetan girl, not yet 20, who said after graduation she would do "what will be best for the country – what the party decides".

This drew the comment: "In the past we had been tempted to dismiss as mere cold-war tactics the solicitude professed by the Chinese government toward colonial or exploited peoples throughout the world. But today's tour obliges us to reconsider the question; for we have witnessed the respectful caution with which the Chinese tackle the problem of their ethnic groups . . .

"Undoubtedly Communist philosophy and strategy have ulterior motives in respecting minorities. But the fact remains that for all practical purposes minorities are better treated under such a philosophy than under Western regimes, where economic considerations take priority over all others."

It was a surprising conclusion to draw in view of the widely reported massacres of Tibetans by the communists a year or two previously, but they said, "far from assimilating these minorities as much as possible . . . the powerful Chinese State does all it can to preserve their national characteristics, and notably their languages".

The group then had a look at industrial China in the region of Manchuria in the north when it visited a factory making sleeping cars for the railroad.

"Heavy industry in China makes us think of a child dressed up in his father's clothes. He seems lost inside them, a bit ludicrous; but he knows the future will take care of all that . . .

"We are convinced that we are witnessing the beginning of an industrial revolution . . . We have no doubt that in a little while – never mind whether it is one year or five – this factory will be filled to bursting with people and machines working in real co-ordination with the single purpose of exceeding their quotas."

When later visiting a carpet factory they concluded: "It is clear that the small-wage earner is no longer a mere pariah, as he was before. They are trying in every possible way to interest him in public affairs, in the new ideology, in the industrial revolution. They have succeeded at least in convincing him that he is no longer just a speck of dust in the proletarian mass, and that he is part of this revolution; that without him China wouldn't be the power it has become in the last eleven years. How could the Chinese worker fail to feel a certain pride? How could he fail to be disconcerted if he could read the unceasing lamentations of Western journalists over the fate of the nameless forced labourers of the New China?

"That there are slave-labour camps is a hypothesis that for obvious reasons we can neither confirm nor deny. What is certain is that the mass of Chinese workers are living better than they ever have before . . .

"The government has given the Chinese a job to do, and *gets them to do it* . . . which is a considerable innovation when you think of the fatalistic and unworldly China of the past.

"One may disagree with the methods used; one may reject the governing principles; one may be repelled at the thought of such a system ever being established in Canada; but in a world dominated by power politics such attitudes are apt to be swept aside as the nice scruples of comfortable people . . . China's methods are going to be imitated by the two-thirds of the human race that goes to bed hungry every night. And the moral indignation of the West will be powerless to stop it.

"China is a country on the march. Of course the Party makes mistakes... of course the people are eventually going to get out of breath from running this relentless race; you only have to think of the refugees arriving every day in Macao and Hong Kong. But any anti-Communist who founded his hopes on this would be crazy. Six hundred and fifty million Chinese are a good part of the world. And the Communist Party isn't out of breath, and it isn't running away. Not it."

The day before the country's national celebration, Trudeau arranged for the group to meet a New Zealand resident in China named Rewi Alley.

Alley was named after Rewi Maniapoto, a great Maori warrior of the last century. Born in 1900, he won a Military Medal in the Great War and tried his hand at sheep farming before leaving for Shanghai in 1927 "for a look". Ten years later he had become a communist while working in the international community in the city, helping to hide partisans of Mao's underground and their radios in his house. He was later to join the New Zealand Communist Party and was credited with bringing it into the Chinese communist fold after the Peking-Moscow split. He was virulently anti-American and saw his home country as a "catspaw of United States imperialism".[9]

Trudeau said he had heard much of Alley when he had visited China in 1949 and wanted very much to meet him. Trudeau and Hébert described him as "no ordinary adventurer. A New Zealander who had been settled in China for more than 30 years he had soon become convinced that the co-operative movement and technical education were essential for the economic liberation of China, and he had organized centres in the most remote districts. After the Communists came to power, he quite naturally continued to live and write in his adopted country.

"He is a thickset, red-haired man with an open and friendly look on his face ... We take advantage of this meeting to clarify certain points about the Chinese mentality ... He paints us a picture of China that is developing prodigiously; that is opening

145

up vast tracts of desert and swamp to agriculture or mining. 'Precisely because of the size of the task and the loftiness of their aims, there are very few abuses. Exemplary conduct is essential for the party members. They even set up opportunities for the people to criticize them severely when they fall short of the high ideals they have set themselves.' "

Alley himself doesn't remember much of Trudeau or Hébert except that "they impressed me as being intelligent people keen to learn".[10]

Then the national day burst forth with millions of jugglers, singers, acrobats, onlookers and dancers. In the evening there was a reception for foreign guests and Trudeau met the Chinese prime minister, Chou En-lai, and shook hands twice with him before going into the great hall where he met the country's top men, including Mao Tse-tung.

"It is a stirring moment: these greybeards, in their ripe old age, embody today the triumph of an idea, an idea that has turned the whole world upside down and profoundly changed the course of human history . . . Mao Tse-tung, one of the great men of the century, has a powerful head, an unlined face, and a look of wisdom tinged with melancholy. The eyes in that tranquil face are heavy with having seen too much of the misery of men."

After the reception they were led outside and Trudeau dashed off into the crowd only to return to the hotel hours later after, apparently, partying with the Chinese crowds.

The group left China in the early hours of Saturday, October 22, when they could see cyclists moving slowly through the fog.

"They are travelling the road of the future, a future so filled with promise and with trials that even the most audacious planners cannot trace its outline."

Touching on international politics, Trudeau and Hébert said "the 'two-China' policy is based on profound ignorance of the Chinese mentality. The accredited anti-communists, of course, will go on believing for the next 50 years that the Chinese are on the verge of rising against their Communist government just as some people have believed the same of the U.S.S.R. for 44 years."[11]

Once out of Peking the group dispersed and Trudeau passed a few days in Russia before leaving Leningrad September 29 for Paris, and eventually Canada.

FOOTNOTES CHAPTER 9

1. Le Devoir, December 6, 1958.
2. Le Devoir, April 11, 1959.
3. Le Devoir, April 13, 1959.
4. Alphonse Gagnon, "En Plein Forme," Les Éditions du Jour, Ottawa, 1961.
5. Theodore Draper, "Castro's Revolution," Frederick A. Praeger Inc., New York, 1967, p. 68.
6. Pierre Elliott Trudeau, "Diefenbaker Monte Un Ballon," Cité Libre, April, 1960.
7. Pierre Elliott Trudeau, "Notes Sure L'Élection Provinciale," Cité Libre, June-July, 1960.
8. Pierre Elliott Trudeau, "L'Élection du 22 Juin 1960," Cité Libre, August-September, 1960.
9. New Zealand Herald, October 26, 1973.
10. From a letter to the author, May 7, 1977.
11. Pierre Elliott Trudeau and Jacques Hébert, "Two Innocents in Red China," translated by I. M. Owen, Oxford University Press, Toronto, 1968.

10

Trudeau and the Liberals

The year 1960 saw an open split in Quebec's left wing over the issue of nationalism when Pierre Bourgault founded the separatist Rassemblement Pour L'Indépendance Nationale.

The first in a series of such movements, it was to find an implacable, articulate enemy in Trudeau.

In another development, the CLCC had finally dropped its Catholic affiliation and become the Confederation of National Trade Unions, after years of work in that direction by Jean Marchand.

René Lévesque, now a cabinet minister, was fighting a battle to swing the Liberal government farther to the left.

Gerard Pelletier recalls a conversation with him and Trudeau in which Lévesque said a prime minister with a decisive majority could act as a virtual despot. Trudeau agreed with him that unless five or six ministers threatened to resign in protest, there was nothing to prevent a prime minister's will being done.[1]

Early in 1961 Trudeau travelled to Ottawa to attend the three-day convention of the national Liberal Party as an observer. He found it a congress for Liberals, not for liberals.

As Trudeau saw it, there was one strategic fact to take into account in federal politics—there were three opposition parties to the incumbent Conservatives—the Liberals, CCF and the

Social Credit Party. The "New Party" had adopted a position sufficiently left-wing and reformist to appeal to the labour unions and with the Conservatives on the right, the Liberals found themselves occupying a thin slice of centre ground.

They thus had three choices: they could continue that way, moving either to the right or left as expediency demanded; they could move to the left and try to take over the New Party's ground, or they could define themselves as the only traditional party able to take power while appealing to the "bourgeois, capitalist loyalties" of the average voter.

It seemed that the party had decided, consciously or unconsciously, on the third choice. Actions taken during the congress had stressed provincial autonomy, and in fact had restructured the national party so that it was a federation of 10 provincial associations.

In their defence and international policies the Liberals hadn't risked being taken for leftists, and while there wasn't any ideology outlined, the party had established itself to the right of centre, as a force to be reckoned with.

"Thus nowhere was there a serious question of economic control, of planned investments, industrial democracy, anti-monopoly measures or a pro-union policy."[2]

It was an important event for the Conservatives, but even more so for the New Party since the Liberals had shown they wouldn't move toward the left. In a time of unemployment, a party which situated itself there would carry a lot of weight.

Trudeau's opening shot in his private war with the separatists came in March that year with an article in Cité Libre entitled "L'Alienation Nationaliste".

What the nationalists and "new" separatists had to realize was that the Canadian constitution as it stood allowed them to realize themselves fully, as French Canadians, within it.

True, the "new" separatists were passing themselves off as socialists and promised that in an independent Quebec the old elites would be banished. But in working for independence against the English, they would have to ally themselves with the old guard which they had just succeeded in getting rid of, because by themselves they weren't strong enough.

149

"Twenty-five years ago, nationalism succeeded in putting all the energies released by the economic crisis of the thirties into the service of reaction. The forces born in the post-war period must not, at all costs, be alienated by neo-nationalism, which is today provoking a new unemployment crisis.

"Open our borders, our people are dying from suffocation!"

In April 1961 the long-awaited event happened when the CCF and the Canadian Labour Congress jointly formed the New Democratic Party, a socialist movement with supposedly broad union support modelled on the Labour Party in England.

But as Trudeau had warned, it was formed before there was a broad coalition of the left in Quebec established, and it seemed foredoomed to the same fate as the old CCF in Quebec: that of being perceived by French Canadians as foreign and English.

It was about the same time that an anthology was published to coincide with the founding of the new party, entitled "Social Purpose for Canada".

In the early thirties, shortly after the CCF had been formed, another anthology called "Social Planning for Canada" had been published to serve in part as a blueprint for future social and economic planning in Canada.

Frank Scott had then been one of the contributors, and almost 30 years later he helped organize the collation and publishing of a similar project to which Trudeau contributed. Others who contributed were Michael Oliver, who also edited the volume, John Porter, Kenneth McNaught and of course Scott. On the editorial board were Oliver, Scott, Dr. Eugene Forsey, David Lewis, George Grube, Professor J. C. Weldon and Thomas Shoyama.

Trudeau had been involved since the board had held its first meeting three years earlier, when funds became available through the Boag Foundation, a trust fund for socialist education.

Trudeau's essay was given the neutral title of "The Practice and Theory of Federalism". But it was not so much a descriptive essay as a distillation of his thoughts on socialist tactics and strategy. In 36 pages he crystallized a plan of action for socialists to take power in Canada through federalism, and urged them to follow it.

"The electoral failings of democratic socialism in most industrial societies have led the partisans of social democracy in recent years to reappraise their ends and their means in the light of changing social and economic reality," he wrote.

"For example, the nationalization of the instruments of production is now being considered less as an end than as a means, and one that might in many cases be replaced by more flexible processes of economic control and redistribution.

"Left-wing thinkers have too often assumed that fundamental reform is impossible without a vast increase, in law or in fact, of the national government's areas of jurisdiction . . . "

Trudeau disagreed and said that assumption had done considerable harm to reform, and claimed that radicalism can more easily be introduced through a federal system than through a centralized one. "Canadian socialists must consider federalism as a positive asset, rather than as an inevitable handicap."

He was really urging socialists to use "greater realism and greater flexibility in the socialist approach to problems of federalism: I should like to see socialists feeling free to espouse whatever political trends or to use whatever constitutional tools happen to fit each particular problem at each particular time . . .

Mao Tse-tung, the Chinese leader he had met a year before, was quoted to show that "revolutionary bases, in spite of their insignificant size, are a great political force . . . revolution and revolutionary wars proceed from birth to development, from small to large, from lack of power to seizure of power.

"In a non-revolutionary society and in non-revolutionary times," continued Trudeau, " . . . democratic reformers must proceed step by step, convincing little bands of intellectuals here, rallying sections of the working class there, and appealing to the underprivileged in the next place. The drive toward power must begin with the establishment of bridgeheads, since at the outset it is obviously easier to convert specific groups or localities than to win over an absolute majority of the whole nation."

A system of proportional representation would be best for the introduction of radical strategy, but failing that, the federal system was the next best system.

"Indeed the experience of that superb strategist Mao Tse-tung might lead us to conclude that in a vast and heterogeneous country, the possibility of establishing socialist strongholds in certain regions is the very best thing.

"Federalism must be welcomed as a valuable tool which permits dynamic parties to plant socialist governments in certain provinces, from which the seed of radicalism can slowly spread."

Trudeau was puzzled by socialist dogmatists who refused to "dilute" their beliefs in various areas. "In terms of political tactics, the only real question democratic socialists must answer is: 'Just how much reform can the majority of the people be brought to desire at the present time?' . . . Socialists must stand for different things in different parts of Canada."

Their refusal to do so had weakened Le Rassemblement, an effort to "enlarge the left in Quebec," and fatally weakened the attempt to form a union of democratic forces.

"Radicalism in different parts of Canada must be implanted in different fashions. For a time, parties with the same name may find themselves preaching policies differing in scope from one province to the other. Perhaps even parties with different names may preach the same ideology in different provinces." It would be a confused time, perhaps, but challenging.

Later he discussed the mechanics of federal-provincial relations and wrote, "the upshot of my entire argument in this section is that socialists, rather than water down (to use a previous expression) their socialism, must constantly seek ways of adapting it to a bicultural society governed under a federal constitution. And since the future of Canadian federalism lies clearly in the direction of co-operation, the wise socialist will turn his thoughts in that direction, keeping in mind the importance of establishing buffer zones of joint sovereignty and co-operative zones of joint administration between the two levels of government."

Trudeau concluded his essay with, "to many an idealist, it

may appear that socialism within a federal structure of government is not as pure, as exciting, and as efficient as socialism in a unitary state.

"That may be so, just as democratic socialism may be less efficient and far-reaching than the totalitarian brand. But just as democracy is a value in itself, which cannot be sacrificed to considerations of expediency, likewise at certain times and in certain places federalism may be held to be a fundamental value, and the penalty for disregarding it may be the complete collapse of socialism itself."

That summer Trudeau traded his thoughts about Mao's revolution for the real thing in Algeria. The National Liberation Front was in the final stages of a bloody war with the French that had lasted seven years when he visited there.

He then travelled to Paris for the annual meeting of the International Political Science Association from September 26 to 30, 1961. It was an association that brought together some familiar names for Trudeau: Oskar Lange, an organizer of the 1952 Moscow economic conference, who was on the executive committee; Michael Oliver, who was scheduled to give a paper on the "political problems of poly-ethnic countries" and Robert McKenzie of the London School of Economics, who gave a paper on "political activities and inner party democracy" in Great Britain.

"He had been globe trotting that summer," McKenzie recalled of Trudeau. He, Oliver and Trudeau had lunch together and talked about the New Democratic Party. Oliver had been involved in the formation of it and McKenzie had been at the founding convention as a journalist the previous April.

McKenzie said Oliver was enthused about the chances of success for the new party, based as it was on union support from the Canadian Labour Congress. Trudeau remained non-committal throughout that conversation, but once Oliver had left, he asked McKenzie his opinion on the new party's chances of success.

He told Trudeau he didn't think the NDP would work as it

was tied too closely to the unions and wouldn't gain any headway in Quebec. As a result, it would probably only win 10 per cent of the popular vote, if that.

"I would be forced," said McKenzie, "probably holding my nose, to join the Liberal Party to try to hold the Canadian political entity together." Years later he met Trudeau, who recalled the conversation, and remarked, "it was a seminal occasion for me".

All that year international tension had been increasing. John F. Kennedy had been elected president of the U.S. and pursued an ideological offensive against communism which led to the abortive Bay of Pigs invasion by a ragtag group of Cuban exiles. In the fall the Russians had started nuclear tests again after a three year lull, and the Americans resumed their test program in response.

Trudeau clearly felt nuclear incineration was a possibility with which to reckon. It would take only 300 atom bombs to wipe out all human life in the U.S. and 4,000 to do the same in the U.S.S.R. But the Americans had a reserve of 75,000 such bombs and the Russians at least half as many. For Trudeau, it was complete madness.

"This unimaginable destructive power is in the service of two enemies who doubtless want peace with all their hearts, but who are ready to instantaneously respond to any aggression."

As the speed of the possible response became faster and faster, the chances of war became greater and greater, and the chances of survival smaller and smaller. Any slight accident, error or miscalculation might launch a nuclear war.

Norbert Weiner had noted in his book "The Human Use of Human Beings" in 1950 that "in the long run there is no distinction between arming ourselves and arming the enemy".

Even in peace time, nuclear tests posed a terrible danger to humans. The Nobel Prize Winner Dr. Linus Pauling had estimated that as a result of the contamination from the explosion of 180 megatons worth of nuclear bombs thus far, 140,000 children around the world had been born "deformed, dwarf-like, mentally retarded or otherwise degenerate".

154

Yet in September 1961, the Russians had started their tests again. "By this cynicism, this cruelty, this moral degeneracy, Khrushchev classified himself at once among the greatest monsters of history... for thanks to his sole 50-megaton bomb, Khrushchev condemned 40,000 children around the world to being born with severe physical or mental handicaps."

What were French Canadians doing about it? Dreaming of a separate Quebec – Laurentia. The English Canadians had formed several groups, including the Canadian Committee for the Control of Radiation Hazards and the Canadian Peace Research Institute.

"Today, youth is resolutely turning its face toward the past and energetically attacking problems whose solutions were found a century ago ...

"It was Nero who was severely judged by history for having played his violin (or something else) while Rome burned. But the damned brood of today could well escape such condemnation; for perhaps man's past won't have a future."[4]

Trudeau decided to back up his words with action and the next spring accepted an invitation to join the board of directors of the Canadian Peace Research Institute.

CAPRI had been founded by Norman Alcock, a Canadian engineer and nuclear physicist who had decided in 1959 to change his lifestyle and dedicate himself to organizing a research institute to analyze war and conflict which "might just discover the political and social inventions needed for a warless world".

The institute was duly incorporated in 1961 and a fund-raising campaign begun in the following year. To help in the campaign, Alcock had recruited a prestigious board including: Dr. Franc R. Joubin, who led in the discovery and development of Canada's uranium ore reserves and who was a director of Guaranty Trust; Dr. Brock Chisholm, a former director of the World Health Organization; Francis Winspear, a millionaire and former head of the Canadian Chamber of Commerce; Trudeau, and Pelletier, who was then editor-in-chief of La Presse. [Gagnon had quit after in-fighting at the newspaper.]

Alcock said he invited Trudeau onto the board because "he

had particular legitimacy in Quebec and a gut feeling for disarmament". Although he turned out to be "the furthest left on the board," he still had "respectability.

"When I first met him he was wearing sandals," Alcock recalled with a smile. "He had this flair for casualness and elegance." He enlivened some of their board meetings when he arrived wearing a cape and proceeded to get into heated discussions with some of the more staid members of the board.

Trudeau wrote the bylaws of the institute and attended several meetings. Despite CAPRI's altruistic motives, it did meet opposition, ironically in the left-wing media.

W. J. Stankiewicz criticized CAPRI in the May, 1962 issue of the Canadian Forum for its "high-pressure methods to recruit door-to-door canvassers". He continued, "the institute has been launched in a way more suited to a Billy Graham crusade than an endeavour with scientific goals.

"Scientific research is best conducted by organizations which guarantee immunity from the pressures of popular opinion, such as the universities or institutes financed through endowments . . . the chances of fulfilling the promises of its founders are very slender indeed."

About the same time, Trudeau organized and launched his main offensive on the separatists and nationalists in Quebec with a special issue of Cité Libre. It was to be the review's best selling edition – 9,500 copies.

Separatists were fond of quoting the aphorism, "good government is no substitute for self-government," he said. But it had to be said that self-government didn't necessarily mean national self-determination. And "good government is a damn good substitute for national self-determination".

He reviewed world history and concluded that the idea of the nation-state "was itself absurd . . . for any national minority which liberates itself will almost invariably find in its heart a new national minority which will have the same right to reclaim its liberty. Thus the chain of revolutions would continue . . . "

Quebec nationalism was merely a small manifestation of a global phenomenon. It had resulted from the attempt by English

Canadians to assimilate them and took the form in some people of separatism, which was nonetheless "an emotional and prejudiced choice, essentially". A second choice was possible for French Canadians – federalism.

If there wasn't a great French Canadian presence federally it was because they had chosen not to get involved. They had preferred to concentrate their energies on a narrow-minded Quebec nationalism which hadn't succeeded in producing any more skilled workmen, richer financiers or more efficient civil servants.

Now there was the new appearance of the separatists distinguished by being totalitarian, anti-semitic and ignorant of basic economics.

"Now this is what I call the new treason of the intellectuals: this self-deluding passion of a large segment of our thinking population for throwing themselves headlong – intellectually and spiritually – into purely escapist pursuits.

"The nation is, in fact, the guardian of certain very positive qualities: a cultural heritage, common traditions, a community awareness, historical continuity, a set of mores, all of which – at this juncture in history – go to make a man what he is. . . . They belong to a transitional period in world history. . . . Except to pinpoint ourselves in the right historical perspective, then, there is not much to be gained in brushing them aside on the ground that the nation of French Canadians will some day fade from view, and that Canada itself will undoubtedly not exist forever.

"The die is cast in Canada: there are two main ethnic and linguistic groups; each is too strong and too deeply rooted in the past, too firmly bound to a mother culture, to be able to engulf the other. But if the two will collaborate at the hub of a truly pluralistic state, Canada could become the envied seat of a form of federalism that belongs to tomorrow's world . . . Canadian federalism is an experiment of major proportions; it could become a brilliant prototype for the moulding of tomorrow's civilization."[5]

Trudeau's friend, René Lévesque, had precipitated a crisis that summer and fall when he pushed for the nationalization of hydro-electric companies against strong opposition from the National Union. To clear the air, and win a decisive mandate, Lesage called an election on the issue for November 16, 1962.

But as the election approached, a disaster appeared imminent for Trudeau, because the left, instead of uniting, was infighting. The NDP had refused to consider the very real possibility that the right might win the next election and "equally refused to consider the usefulness, from the point of view of democracy and progress of a victory by the sole left-winger who could take power – René Lévesque".

Some NDPers had been heard to say that the only important thing for the party in the election was to be seen as an "authentic party of the left". It had even gone so far as to put up a candidate against René Lévesque.

If the NDP ran some candidates and managed to win a few seats, it would only serve to show how weak they really were. On the other hand, they could end up not winning any seats but splitting the vote sufficiently so that the right would regain power again. "In one way or the other, the socialists would have succeeded in showing their complete incompetence, in so far as their plan of action went, by their strategy."

The NDP in Quebec was "so preoccupied with being the only left and so envious of being the whole left, that it has completely forgotten the necessity of first creating a left and increasing its ranks. What strikes me particularly, is that it takes its exclusivity for revolutionary purity, while it's only pure ignorance.

"If our intellectuals had read a little Marx, Lenin and Mao Tse-tung, they would know that true revolutionaries are ready to accept a tactical compromise if necessary to allow a still-young left to come into the world."

That was why Britain's Labour Party and Saskatchewan's provincial CCF party had grown strong – they had understandings with the Liberal parties. "Later, when the left existed, when it was numerous, when it had deep roots, it could let itself elaborate strategies that were a little more independent...as a French militant recalled: 'we're on the left, but no farther.' "

Then, for the first time, Trudeau had something positive to

say about the Quebec Liberal Party. Although it had rejected Jean Marchand as a candidate for the party, it was still sufficiently open "to have named a man of the left as a minister in 1960" (René Lévesque) and was "progressive enough to dare to lay its life on the line in 1962 over a question raised by this same minister".[6]

It must have been this kind of article, where Marx was quoted, that enraged conservatives in the province. In mid-August a letter had been circulated to colleges, convents, seminaries and universities urging authorities not to let Cité Libre be distributed on their grounds. It was signed by J.-G. Bleau, of the Via Veritas Vita, a lay French Canadian group based in Ville d'Anjou.

"Cité Libre, after having been studied and scrutinized from the first issue by members of the V.V.V. best versed in philosophy and theology, has been judged to be leftist, and tending toward Marxism, materialism, neutralism, liberalism and paganism.

"The publication 'Cité Libre' has never hidden the fact that it's a review of the Left, in the classical sense attributed to the word 'Left'. Members of the V.V.V. have learned, through numerous leftist authors, that the Left is only a great open road to the Extreme Left which isn't anything other than integral communism, atheist Marxism. . . . such as it exists behind the iron and bamboo curtains. More, members of the V.V.V. . . . have gathered evidence that the said review, Cité Libre, published in Montreal, counts among its editors avowed anti-clerics, agnostics, fellow travelling Marxists and writers whose ideas identify them with those of international freemasonry."[7]

Cité Libre received a copy of the letter from an unnamed clergyman and reprinted it, with only a postscript: "the above document isn't a joke, at least not in the minds of its authors."

That September Trudeau ended a long flirtation with the University of Montreal when he joined the Research Institute of Public Law. The institute's first director was Jean Beetz, who was appointed after its formation at Paul Gérin-Lajoie's initiative.

Another French Canadian member of the institute was Marc Lalonde, who had been an executive assistant to the Conservative minister of justice. Lalonde had contributed to Cité Libre and was close enough to it to eventually become a member of one of its administrative committees, and not surprisingly asked his friend Trudeau to join the institute.

Phillip Garigue, the dean of the faculty of social science at the university, and another old alumnus of the LSE, had tried in vain to hire him as a full time professor before. "I approached him at least twice and I was turned down twice," he recalled. "He wasn't sure he wanted to become a full-time professor. He had many other things he wanted to do, so when he received an offer to act as a part-time professor in the faculty of law he preferred that."

So at the age of 43, Trudeau seemed to settle into the academic life of his old university. It was not the university he had known, however. Radical separatists had taken over the student newspaper he had once edited, Quartier Latin, and he found himself in the situation of being regarded, ironically, as an establishment stooge, a reactionary.

A colleague recalls Trudeau being present at a student political meeting where a "federalist sell-out" was referred to as "a pierre elliott trudeau". In that environment, he began to feel isolated.

It was ironic for Trudeau to be labelled a reactionary, for it was later claimed by Pelletier that he had been prevented from joining any faculty for years because he was considered too radical.

Dr. Donatien Marion, who had been a member of the university's board of governors from 1950 to 1955, recalled a meeting in which Trudeau's appointment to the faculty of law was vetoed.

The board secretary, Marcel Faribault, read Trudeau's name and received no objection from any of the governors. But the candidate had to receive the approval of the chancellor, and he was Paul Émile Cardinal Leger, the patron of Nos Cours, which had published the criticism of Trudeau's Moscow series in Le Devoir.

According to Marion, Leger said "in the present circum-

160

stances, I think it would be better not to make this nomination, given the alleged pro-communist opinions of Mr. Trudeau".[8]

But Marion's version may be suspect, as Léon Lortie, the official historian of the university, said "Dr. Donatien Marion was the most anti-liberal man on the board". He was pro-Duplessis, very conservative and a member of the secret nationalist society, the Order of Jacques Cartier.

Lortie said "nothing was ever written down in the minutes of meetings [about turning down candidates]. There was never anything on paper – I think it was done by telephone. I'm sure he was refused as a professor at least once."

Cardinal Leger, for his part, denied the allegation outright,[9] and there the matter rests, still clouded.

In the fall of 1962 Trudeau, Pelletier and Marchand all had a long look at themselves and their futures. In the June 18 election the NDP, far from increasing its vote with its allegedly broad power base, actually dropped six seats to 19. The Liberals had gained a substantial number of seats, but only enough to force the Conservatives into a minority government position.

Pelletier recalled that the NDP wasn't then perceived as having any French Canadian element and that "the national direction of the party was so accident-prone – they were always blundering". He remembered the comment of a B.C. member who said he believed in bilingualism, so long as everyone spoke English. Then there was the towering, maverick NDP MP Douglas Fisher, who had equated French Canadian culture with hockey star Rocket Richard and stripper Lili St. Cyr.

Marchand, who had succeeded in rising to the top of the CLCC, (and later CNTU) and changing it fundamentally to make it non-denominational and highly militant, wanted to do the same with the Liberal Party, recalled Pelletier.

"Marchand said, 'that's the way we must proceed in politics – we must not be seen to come from the outside.'"

To top it all off, the NDP was adopting a two-nations formula for Canada, which the three thought could only lead to disaster. So by the beginning of 1963, they were ready to listen to an expected offer by Maurice Lamontagne to join the Liberal Party.

But fate intervened on January 12, 1963, when Pearson was

speaking to the York-Scarborough Liberal Association. In a sudden, unexpected move, he reversed the stand of his party and caucus and supported nuclear weapons for Canada.

For the two board members of CAPRI, Trudeau and Pelletier, it was too much, and they resolved not to join the Liberals. And without them, there was no chance Marchand would join either.

Not only did Trudeau decide not to join the Liberals, but he began to actively campaign for the New Democratic Party. On the evening of March 26 he spoke at an NDP rally for Thérèse Casgrain and Charles Taylor, two socialist candidates in the ridings of Outremont-St. Jean and Mont-Royal respectively, to a crowd 400-strong.

An account of his speech in La Presse the next day was headed, "Pearson became a 'turn-coat' and all the rest followed (Trudeau).

"In his first shattering speech from the NDP hustings," the article continued, "Mr. Pierre Elliott Trudeau . . . last night violently attacked the Liberal Party, which he denounced because of its leader, Mr. Lester B. Pearson, whom he called an 'unfrocked priest of peace' . . . the political immorality of the party's leaders and members . . . and the docility and servility of the provincial Liberal Party . . . "

Trudeau was quoted as saying, "After six years in opposition the Liberal Party hasn't reformed itself. It's composed of docile, obedient young Liberals, of a cynical, disillusioned old guard and, between those two, a group of my generation who drool with anticipation in seeing the proximity of power."

Soon afterwards he followed up on the theme of this speech in a Cité Libre article entitled "Pearson – or the Abdication of the Spirit". In it he heaped scorn on the Liberal Party, its leader, members and principles – or lack of them. Not only that, but he published the article in the same month as another federal election and announced he would vote for the NDP.

Trudeau must have believed the article would block forever his entering the Liberal Party.

He made it clear at the start that he wasn't questioning the

Liberals' nuclear policy per se, but examining the "anti-demo-cratic reflexes" of the "Liberal herd". At the Liberal convention he had attended January 13, 1961, Pearson and the party had stated their opposition to the acquisition or use of nuclear weapons. In January the next year, and again on April 30, 1962, Pearson reiterated the same policy. It was re-stated yet again on November 14, 1962, when "the official program of the Liberal Party still remained, then, opposed to the presence of nuclear arms on Canadian soil".

But on the morning of January 12, 1963, all that changed. Pearson argued that if the CF-104 jet fighters and Bomarc missiles weren't given nuclear bombs and warheads, it would be a waste of $750 million.

"One is tempted to ask our Nobel Peace Prizewinner what would happen to peace if the U.S.A. and the Soviet Union shared this concern for money, and also refused to renounce the use of certain arms on the grounds that they had cost them a lot of cash . . . ?"

All that Pearson had to do to put himself in a good position to gain power was to "betray the program of his party as well as the idealism with which he has always been identified. Fund raisers promised to be generous. And Gallup showed that a pro-nuclear arms policy would not wipe out a majority of voters. Power offered itself to Mr. Pearson: he had nothing to lose except his honour. He lost it. And his entire party lost it with him.

"Even if I was completely favourable to nuclear arms, even if Mr. Pearson was right to change his personal ideas, I would still denounce the autocracy of the Liberal structure and the extraordinary cowardice of its members.

"I don't remember having seen, since I started studying politics, a spectacle more degrading than the one of all these Liberals turning their coats in unison with the chief, when they saw a chance to take power."

Trudeau railed at the "dictatorship of the chief" and scorned the Liberal Youth, the National Association and National Federation of Liberal University Students, for falling into line after Pearson's abrupt change of policy.

"Once the head of the herd showed the way, the rest followed along with all the elegance of cattle rushing to the trough.

"Thus the political philosophy of the Liberal Party is quite simple: 'say anything, think anything; or better still, don't think anything at all; but put us in power because we're the ones who can best govern you.'"

Pearson and the Liberals believed that "the most serious questions only have the importance that's attached to them by votes; and there doesn't seem to be in this party a single man any more for whom principles are more important than political power.

"It is sad to think that not too long ago these new arrivals to power were scandalized and trembling with indignation because the National Union bought votes with frigidaires. But of those who buy votes with betrayed principles . . . ?

"In the name of efficiency and realism I have had to betray, God forgive me, certain rebellions of youth from time to time. But as yet I haven't agreed to trample on democracy. That's why, in the April 8 elections, I intend to vote for the New Democratic Party.

"I think it's also the duty of all those who believe it's urgent to block the current of Canadian political thought that is leading to absolute degradation. Government instability, the fragmentation of the opposition, the risk of 'losing one's vote', these are all minor dangers compared to the spiritual abdication to which Pearson is leading us."[10]

Despite Trudeau's intervention, things went from bad to worse for the NDP in the election. Both Taylor and Casgrain lost, the party failed to win a single seat in Quebec, and in fact lost two seats nationally.

The Liberals had gathered enough seats nationally to form a minority government and although they didn't win one seat in Saskatchewan they cut the Social Credit Party back to six seats in Quebec.

In the month after the election Trudeau helped form the Ligue Pour Les Droits de L'Homme, or the Quebec Civil Liberties Association, with Michael Oliver, Frank Scott, Casgrain and her first cousin, Raymond Boyer, Jean-Louis Gagnon, Léon Patenaude, Jacques Hébert and Jean Marchand.

While most citizens in Quebec and Canada were expressing their political convictions through the federal election, there was a tiny group of extremists who decided to go the violent route. They called themselves the Front for the Liberation of Quebec. The quiet of Montreal streets was shattered by exploding bombs in trash cans and mail boxes, leaving shattered bystanders in their wake.

The terrorists of the FLQ wanted independence immediately, and they had sworn to bring it about through blood, not the ballot box.

Trudeau responded to the wave of separatism in part with another essay, "Federalism, Nationalism and Reason". "If the heavy paste of nationalism is relied upon to keep a unitary nation-state together, much more nationalism would appear to be required in the case of a federal nation-state. Yet if nationalism is encouraged as a rightful doctrine and noble passion, what is to prevent it from being used by some group, region or province within the nation?

"The answer, of course, is that no amount of logic can prevent such an escalation.

"One way of offsetting the appeal of separatism is by investing tremendous amounts of time, energy, and money in nationalism, at the federal level. A national image must be created that will have such an appeal as to make any image of a separatist group unattractive. Resources must be diverted into such things as national flags, anthems, education, arts councils, broadcasting corporations, film boards; the territory must be bound together by a network of railways, highways, airlines; the national culture and the national economy must be protected by taxes and tariffs; ownership of resources and industry by nationals must be made a matter of policy. In short, the whole of the citizenry must be made to feel that it is only within the framework of the federal state that their language, culture, institutions, sacred traditions and standard of living can be protected from external attack and internal strife."

But if this nationalism didn't fulfill the aspirations of a minority, or the demands of the minority became too much, "a critical point can be reached beyond which separatism takes place, or a civil war is fought".

Then, "no amount of nationalism, however great, can save the federation. Any expenditure of emotional appeal . . . at the national level will only serve to justify similar appeals at the regional level, where they are just as likely to be effective. Thus the great moment of truth arrives when it is realized that in the last resort the mainspring of federalism cannot be emotion but must be reason.

"If politicians must bring emotions into the act, let them get emotional about functionalism!

"But in the advanced societies . . . where the road to progress lies in the direction of international integration, nationalism will have to be discarded as a rustic and clumsy tool."[11]

Trudeau's battle with the separatists wasn't confined to learned treatises. It extended to the magazine he had helped found and nurtured for more than a decade, Cité Libre.

In late 1963, to introduce some fresh blood into the magazine, two young French Canadians named Jean Pellerin and Pierre Vallières were invited to join the editorial board.

But as Jacques Hébert noted, "Pierre Vallières had hidden his separatism quite well—no one suspected him and he was elected editor".

Within months Cité Libre had become a nationalist, separatist mouthpiece almost indistinguishable from the separatist, revolutionary magazine Parti Pris.

"It was a coup," said Hébert. "The first edition was against everything we stood for."

Trudeau and his friends refused to take it lying down and told Vallières and Pellerin to be ready to hand over a statement of their aims to a meeting of the magazine's administrative committee in mid-March. Vallières refused and resigned, taking 13 other contributors with him.

The old group of Cité Libristes pitched in and rebounded in the next issue. Trudeau lashed Vallières and his clique in an article entitled "Les Séparatistes: Des Contre-Révolutionnaries".

"I get so fed up when I hear our nationalist brood calling itself revolutionary. Quebec's revolution, if it had taken place, would first have consisted in freeing man from collective coercions: freeing the citizens brutalized by reactionary and arbitrary governments . . . freeing workers exploited by an oligarchic capitalism . . . But this revolution never took place.

"Around 1960 it seemed that freedom was going to triumph in the end . . . In 1960, everything was becoming possible in Quebec, even revolution. In fact revolution would probably not have been necessary, so wide open was the road to power for all those who had mastered the sciences and the techniques of the day . . . Only it required boldness, intelligence and work. Alas, freedom proved to be too heady a drink to pour for the French Canadian youth of 1960. Almost at the first sip it went at top speed in search of some more soothing milk, some new dogmatism. . . . it took refuge in the bosom of its mother, the Holy Nation.

"For humanity, progress is the slow journey toward personal freedom. Those responsible for a sudden reversal of this course can be defined as counter-revolutionaries.

"Certainly there are historical cases in which personal freedom has scarcely been protected at all by established institutions; it has been possible, then, for a genuine revolutionary to stress collective freedom as a preliminary to personal freedom: Castro, Ben Bella, Lenin . . .

"But when personal freedom exists, it would be inconceivable that a revolutionary should destroy it in the name of some collective ideology. For the very purpose of a collective system is better to ensure personal freedom. (Or else you are a fascist.)

"The fact is that at bottom the separatists despair of ever being able to convince the public of the rightness of their ideas. That long work of education and persuasion among the masses undertaken by the unions for many decades – for this the separatists have neither the courage, nor the means, nor especially, that respect for the other man's freedom which is essential in undertaking it and leading it to success.

"So they want to abolish it and impose a dictatorship of their minority . . . There are numbers of them in the editorial rooms of our newspapers, they swarm at the CBC and the National Film Board, they press with all their weight (?) on the mass media, but still they find the place given them in this society unfair.

"The truth is that the separatist counter-revolution is the work of a powerless petit-bourgeois minority afraid of being left behind by the twentieth-century revolution. Rather than carving themselves out a place in it by ability, they want to make the whole tribe return to the wigwams by declaring its independence.

"Some of the counter-revolutionaries deceive themselves by dressing up in Marxist-Leninist disguises, as has already been done by those African chieftains whom, indeed, they take as models.

"Separatism a revolution? My eye. A counter-revolution; the national-socialist counter-revolution."[12]

In late April, Trudeau traded the infighting and counter-revolution of Cité Libre for a revolution further south – Cuba.

His friend Michel Chartrand had been a state guest there the year before and had enjoyed his visit immensely. When Chartrand had returned to Canada he gave Trudeau's name to Julio Gonzales, the Cuban consul in Montreal, as another French Canadian who would be interested in visiting Cuba.

In the spring of 1964, Gonzales invited a group of seven or eight Canadians to attend the May Day celebrations in Cuba, and included Trudeau, who in turn invited Pierre Carrignan, his colleague at the law faculty.

So Trudeau, Carrignan and his wife travelled south to the sun for eight or nine days. They had originally been invited for three weeks, but had to return home early because of work commitments.

Trudeau was up to his old tricks in Cuba, Carrignan recalled. "At certain times, instead of following the group, he disappeared. You couldn't ask him to follow a group and say to him, be there at two, or go to sleep at five. He wanted to see things for himself and he knew Spanish and could talk to the people, so what he did was just that." The guides and interpreters who accompanied the group wherever it went, weren't disturbed.

"The guides said, 'well, Trudeau is off by himself, let's forget about him,' and we left to visit what we had to visit. You know, the Cubans are communists, but they're Latin communists, and that's a different kind of communist from the Chinese or Russian.

"He was impressed with what had been done in a very short span of time in the field of education," said Carrignan, although Trudeau also noted that the schools were highly politicized.

Carrignan remembers Trudeau saying, "when a country has an immense job to do, and do rapidly, it's almost impossible to do without making fanatics out of the people, without instilling a revolutionary fervour."

They saw some of that fervour during a rally of 200,000 Cubans on May 1 when Fidel Castro spoke for one and a half hours in 110 degree heat.

"There were no elections in Cuba, but when you see something like that you wonder what the need is for elections. The people were going crazy. You can't pay people to act that way," said Carrignan. He thought their spirit was helped by the sight of American ships slowly cruising offshore in the blockade the U.S. had imposed on Cuba.

Soon after May Day Trudeau returned to Montreal where a manifesto jointly authored by himself and six others was just being published in Cité Libre.

He had gathered together the six previously and formed a committee for political realism. They were: Albert Breton, an assistant professor of economics at the University of Montreal; his brother Raymond, in the department of sociology at McGill University; Claude Bruneau, a lawyer with Steinberg's legal department; Yvon Gauthier, a psychoanalyst with Ste. Justine Hospital in Montreal; Maurice Pinard, also of the sociology department at McGill University and Marc Lalonde, a board member at the Institute of Public Law with Trudeau.

The manifesto took the form of "An Appeal for Realism in

Politics" by the seven who were "opposed to the present state of affairs in Canada generally, and in our province in particular".

In a time of high unemployment, it was "inconceivable that politicians should continue to dread budgetary deficits and that, even when resorting to them, they should continue to pay homage to the sacred cow of a balanced budget".

Not only that, but "the present distribution of wealth and income among the various social groups and diverse regions of Canada is plainly unacceptable.

"Our penal system belongs to the middle ages. Our laws are so made that they tend mainly to punish the culprit, seldom to rehabilitate him.

"Justice has become iniquitous in two respects: it is too slow and too expensive.

"We deplore the absence of political leadership in political affairs. Public figures, federal and provincial, do not provide the people with a clear idea of the direction in which they want the country to go. They appear to be the toys of the communications media and of their ghost writers ... our political leaders want to be all things to all men. They propose goals so vague and incoherent that the voters can never be sure of the relationship between what is said today and done tomorrow.

"Democratic progress requires the ready availability of true and complete information. In this way, people can objectively evaluate their Government's policies. To act otherwise is to give way to despotic secrecy.

"The opposition parties must accept their share of the responsibility for keeping the public so little and so badly informed. The Opposition is supposed to force the Government to define their policies and to furnish the public with all relevant information. The Opposition is supposed to proclaim the true problems of the people, for it is the conscience of the Government. Whole sections of society could be completely ignored if the Opposition prostitutes its functions for the sake of short-term political advantage.

"At the same time, however, the present state of our parliamentary mechanism is such that the Opposition, even when it is vigilant, is virtually helpless in the face of the resources available to the Government. The system must be reformed to give the Opposition at state expense the tools which are necessary for it to fulfill its important and true role.

"The lack of information about defence matters released to the public is very worrying and could prove to be a serious setback to democracy in our country. The excuse of 'state secret,' so often a cloak for administrative ineptitude and confusion, can also hide base servility."

Then there was Canada and its constitution. "We do not attach to its existence any sacred or eternal meaning, but it is an historical fact. To take it apart would require an enormous expenditure of energy and gain no proven advantage. It would be to run away from the real and important tasks that lie ahead. To want to integrate it into another geographical entity would also be, it seems to us, a futile task at the present time, even though such a development might appear in principle to conform to the natural course of the world's evolution.

"The most valid trends today are toward more enlightened humanism, toward various forms of political, social and economic universalism. Canada is a reproduction on a smaller and simpler scale of this universal phenomenon. The challenge is for a number of ethnic groups to learn to live together . . . If Canadians cannot make a success of a country such as theirs, how can they contribute in any way to the elaboration of humanism, to the formulation of the international political structures of tomorrow? To confess one's inability to make Canadian Confederation work is, at this stage of history, to admit one's unworthiness to contribute to the universal order.

"If this country is to work, federalism must be preserved and refined at all costs."[12]

On the federal scene the Conservative Party was in a state of chaos, and the Liberal Party only a little less so. Diefenbaker's 12 MPs from Quebec threatened to bolt from the party and cross the floor while Pearson's government had been shaken by successive scandals.

Nevertheless, Pearson believed the Conservatives were in such disarray that a snap election would catch them off guard and win the Liberals a much-desired majority

The Liberals' Quebec wing had been decimated in scandals and Lamontagne cast about over the summer of 1965 for replacements. One man the party wanted was Victor Goldbloom, a hard working, much respected Montreal pediatrician who was a vice-president of the Quebec College of Physicians and Surgeons.

He had been frustrated in trying to bring about some health reforms in the province and decided that to accomplish anything he would have to get into politics. Goldbloom had travelled to Quebec City to see what the chances were of running provincially, but when he was returning to Montreal on the train he ran into Jean Marchand, and they arranged to have breakfast together.

"I've started putting a team together and all the people I have so far are French Canadians," Marchand told Goldbloom.[14] "I'm looking for people who are fluently bilingual and who have deep roots in Quebec ... and who would like to work for the unity of Canada. Would you like to be part of it?"

Goldbloom thought about it and later phoned Marchand to accept and was put in touch with Bob Giguère, the Liberal organizer in Quebec.

Marchand's recruiting efforts were a result of the persuasiveness of Lamontagne and Giguère over the summer.

Lamontagne was really after Marchand as a candidate, but the latter refused to consider the idea unless Trudeau and Pelletier also came along. That presented quite a problem as they had alienated many Liberals with their past pronouncements and writings.

Negotiations dragged on and the three still hadn't decided to run when Pearson called an election on September 1, for November 8.

Time was short, the schedule tight, the issues critical.

Trudeau had to make a decision.

FOOTNOTES CHAPTER 10

1. From an interview with Gerard Pelletier, in Paris, October 12, 1977.

2. Pierre Elliott Trudeau, "À L'Ouest Rien de Nouveau," Cité Libre, February, 1961.

3. Pierre Elliott Trudeau, "The Practice and Theory of Federalism," in "Federalism and the French Canadians," Macmillan of Canada, Toronto, 1968.

4. Pierre Elliott Trudeau, "La Guerre! La Guerre!," Cité Libre, December, 1961.

5. Pierre Elliott Trudeau, "La Nouvelle Trahison des Clercs," Cité Libre, April, 1962. Taken in translation from "Quebec States Her Case," Frank Scott and Michael Oliver, editors, Macmillan of Canada, Toronto, 1964.

6. Pierre Elliott Trudeau, "L'Homme de Gauche et Les Élections Provinciales," Cité Libre, November, 1962.

7. This letter appeared in its entirety in the October, 1962 edition of Cité Libre.

8. From a letter by Dr. Marion in Le Devoir, May 29, 1968.

9. From a letter to the author, July 5, 1977.

10. Pierre Elliott Trudeau, "Pearson—Ou L'Abdication de L'Esprit," Cité Libre, April, 1963.

11. Pierre Elliott Trudeau, "Federalism, Nationalism and Reason," in "The Future of Canadian Federalism," P.-A. Crépeau and C. B. McPherson, editors, University of Toronto Press, Toronto, 1965.

12. Pierre Elliott Trudeau, "Les Séparatistes: Des Contre-Révolutionnaires," Cité Libre, May, 1964. Taken here in translation from the Canadian Forum, July, 1964.

13. Pierre Elliott Trudeau, "An Appeal For Realism in Politics," Cité Libre, May, 1964. Taken here in translation from the May, 1964 edition of Canadian Forum.

14. From an interview with Dr. Victor Goldbloom, July 31, 1977.

11

Power

Shortly before 4 p.m. on Friday, September 10, 1965, Pelletier and Marchand sauntered into the Mount Royal Hotel where a press conference had been called.

Ten minutes later Trudeau entered and they sat down along with Guy Favreau, Pearson's Quebec lieutenant, Lamontagne and Maurice Sauvé, Pearson's minister of forestry, who also had been active in the negotiations.

The three then explained why they had decided to join the Liberal Party and run for election.

"I think it's only normal," said Trudeau, "after spending 15 years as a critic in the role of a critic, after telling others what to do, to try and get out and do it myself. I should try to do something. I should turn from examination to direct action.

"Now, why the Liberals? I believe that is a question I must explain in terms of priorities. When one has a plan, one has to follow an axis of priorities. Our people, the French Canadians, have neither the time, nor the energy, nor the inclination to finance too many revolutions. We must try to choose."

Favreau then got up to welcome the three into the party. Ironically, he said, "Marchand, Pelletier and Trudeau are not people whose arms you twist".

It was ironic, because if any arm twisting had been done, it was by those three. Negotiations had been deadlocked less than

24 hours before when Favreau, Lamontagne and Giguère had explained for four hours why they hadn't wanted Pelletier and Trudeau. Sauvé retired into a bedroom with those two and Marchand and said they should force the other three into accepting them by calling a press conference to announce that they wanted to join the Liberal Party. Favreau and the other two didn't really have any choice and in fact he only agreed to be present at the conference after first refusing.[1]

Lamontagne later claimed he wasn't concerned by the conditions under which the "three wise men," as they were dubbed, entered the party.

"They were the ones who had to compromise when they came into the party."[2]

Reaction to Trudeau's move by his friends was immediate and uncomplimentary. His own magazine disagreed with the move.

"The decision taken by Messrs. Jean Marchand, Gerard Pelletier and Pierre Elliott Trudeau to join the ranks of the Liberal Party has deceived the present editorial board of Cité Libre.

"They are participating in an election which one of them has said was called through 'electoral opportunism'. They're shutting their eyes to the party's past because they consider that there is an 'urgency' in the fact that the very principle of confederation is now in danger.

"But isn't it to be feared that the Quebec left is being divided by the fact that three of its members now find themselves in an ambiguous situation? . . . Finally, isn't it to be feared that by their decision, these three men are creating a confrontation with the country's two separatisms, thus precipitating a state of 'urgency' which they will want to ward off?"

Lastly, the board said it "absolutely disagreed" with the three who apparently believed that there was neither an alternative to separatism or federalism nor room for a third party, the NDP, in Canadian federal politics.[3]

Pierre Vadboncoeur, Trudeau's old friend, had become increasingly nationalist and "was appalled" at his decision to join the Liberals. "It was, in my view, taking the easy way, and doomed to fall into the grip of reactionary forces on all fronts.

He tried to do it the quick way instead of working for the next generation. He couldn't fool the Liberal Party—the Liberal Party fooled him."

Jean-Louis Gagnon thought it was a "clever move" and the logical result of increasing political involvement for Trudeau. "He first started Cité Libre, which was almost a political movement in itself. Then he got involved with Le Rassemblement, which wasn't a party but close to it. In 1963 he was actively campaigning for Casgrain and Taylor for the NDP and then he took the final step."

Fundamentally Trudeau had joined the Liberal Party so that "he could appoint people and he could be in a position to influence policy. Is it not better to achieve 75 per cent of your beliefs than nothing at all?"

Thérèse Casgrain, who would run against Maurice Lamontagne in the election, thought the three "saw themselves as a Trojan horse". Trudeau was merely following the plan he had laid out in his essay "The Practice and Theory of Federalism". "He decided to get in and work from the inside," she said.

Reginald Boisvert, a long-time member of the socialist party and one of the stalwarts of Cité Libre said the decision "troubled me quite a lot. It was a real shock." It troubled him so much, in fact, that he felt compelled to run for the NDP in the 1965 election.

But the criticism and acrimony levelled at Trudeau were the least of his problems, as Claude Ryan noted in an editorial in Le Devoir September 24.

"Fifteen days have passed since the famous September 10 press conference. There is still nothing clear on the horizon. Of all the riding organizations which could have been interested in supporting the candidatures of these two converts [Trudeau and Pelletier], none has so far raised its voice.

"One finds the following paradox. Two men, after having declared that they only wanted to become candidates through a democratic process, are reduced to depending on corridor conferences feverishly pursued in the vice-regal suite of the Windsor Hotel for their fates!

"Regardless of what they have written on the subject in the past, Messrs. Trudeau and Pelletier seem to be stuck, at the start of their political careers, in the far from pleasant slime of conventions 'packed' in advance. That's too unusual for one to pretend that he didn't notice it.

"The man who wants to become active in the heart of an organized party doesn't content himself, ordinarily, with drawing room conversations in the company of Mr. Maurice Lamontagne, Mr. Guy Favreau or Mr. Maurice Sauvé. He begins, on the contrary, by settling down somewhere, by firmly establishing roots in a given milieu . . . If he's a worthwhile man, he ends up being wanted by the people.

"But in the case of our two friends, it's the opposite that has happened. They are blessed from the top first, then they behave as if the mountain should come to them."

Charles Taylor, the NDP candidate for whom Trudeau had campaigned in the 1963 election, had been one of the members of Cité Libre who had signed the editorial against him. Five days after Ryan's editorial, Taylor carried his views into the pages of Le Devoir as well.

"What does one have to think in seeing Pelletier, Marchand and Trudeau form a common front with the Liberals—three men who were counted as among the most lucid of the left program?

"One perhaps could think they had ambitions to try their hands at the helm of the Liberal Party to reorient it toward the left." But that was not a reasonable thought, because who were the possible allies for the left in the party? There was virtually no left except perhaps Pauline Jewett or Judy LaMarsh.

A more serious problem, however, was that for the party to have a leftist program, the very foundations of the party's power base would have to be restructured. It would have to accept the loss of all the money, prestige, press, radio and television of its traditional supporters.

"The unconvincing explanations of these three have caused real anguish among all the elements of the left."

About the same day that Ryan's editorial appeared, Victor Goldbloom learned from Favreau and Lamontagne that he could run in the riding of Mount Royal. But two days after that, he learned from a radio broadcast that Trudeau was also going to run in that riding.

"I called Marchand and he was very upset," said Goldbloom. "He called Lamontagne and Favreau and he was told there just weren't enough ridings to go around." The only thing Marchand could promise Goldbloom was that there would be no outside influence in the nomination convention.

Goldbloom believes Marchand was sincere, but then Marchand didn't draw up the list of delegates to the convention. "Whoever drew up that list had some purpose in mind," said Goldbloom. While the English-to-French population ratio in Mount Royal riding was 85 per cent to 15 per cent, about half the delegates were French Canadian.

Gus Bennett, a member of the executive of the riding's Liberal Association, recalled a meeting of the executive in a downtown lawyer's office one night shortly before the nomination convention.

Bennett says he was told "It's going to be Trudeau and that's all there is to it.

"I said no way—we've got to keep this open. A lot of people were committed" to other candidates. One of the senior association officials "was mad that he might not be able to deliver Trudeau. And I was mad too—so mad I wrote to Pearson saying we had to keep our association democratic.

"Up to that time there were only 32 paid-up members in the Mount Royal Liberal Association. But they packed that hall for the nomination convention. There were a lot of strangers present. Thirty-two members suddenly went to close to 4,000 in a matter of weeks." He said extra application forms for association membership were printed up and only made available to specific persons. "There was a lot of manipulation about who was going to be a delegate. They didn't have to do this. I think Trudeau would have won hands down anyway."

Shortly after that late-night meeting, Bennett organized an all-candidates meeting at the Côte St. Luc School which Trudeau attended.

"He came down to the first meeting and it was a disaster. His shirt was open almost to the navel and he arrived in a sports roadster with golf clubs sticking out. He looked like a hippie. His attitude was, 'if you want me, I'm available'."

After the meeting, Bennett, a friend and Trudeau adjourned to a nearby café where they took a booth. Bennett said his friend, Norman Craig, told Trudeau, "The first thing you've got to do is to get rid of the fruit [Beatle] boots. You've got to clean your act up." Trudeau dutifully did as he was told, and easily won the nomination convention the night of October 7 in the Mount Royal Town Hall.

Afterwards, Bennett said he mentioned to Trudeau that there might have been some questionable delegates at the convention and asked what would he do if he found out it had been fixed. He replied, "If I thought this convention was rigged I'd walk out right now".

Trudeau and Pelletier thought it was high time they explained their actions further and they jointly wrote an article entitled "Trudeau and Pelletier Explain Themselves", which was printed in the October issue of Cité Libre and in Le Devoir, October 12.

"It must never be forgotten that in the democracies that we know, the political party isn't an end but a means, not a goal, but an instrument. He who enters a political party, then, is choosing a tool.

"In the present case, the undersigned are still following the same goals, they are continuing to adhere to the same political ideologies that they have for a long time set forth in Cité Libre: a constitutionalism respectful of the rights of groups and individuals, a democracy aligned with social progress, a federalism which knows how to reconcile a strong, central power with progressive and autonomous provinces, finally, politics open to the left.

"Nevertheless, in the pursuance of these goals, the authors have opted for a means—the federal Liberal Party—which has caused some surprise."

They said their decision to become involved in active politics was merely an extension of their intellectual involvement for the past 15 years. While they had always been more involved with the provincial scene than the federal, the situation had now changed. Quebec had become strong and the central government had become weak, which was why they had to lend their efforts at the federal level, in part to offset provincial and nationalist power in Quebec. They had chosen the Liberal Party, because in Canada there was a certain urgency in fighting anti-federalist tendencies.

"For us, there hasn't been any rupture, we don't repudiate any of our convictions. We have only resolved to pursue elsewhere and in other ways, the intellectual and social struggle which has always claimed us."

Charles Taylor felt betrayed by Trudeau. Here was the man who had worked with him on the NDP hustings and in Cité Libre, but who had joined the Liberals, and who was now going to run against him in the same riding.

The paradox, he said, was that while Trudeau claimed that he hadn't repudiated any of his convictions, he had "joined the least democratic political structure in the country, the federal Liberal Party".[4]

In becoming a "convert" only weeks before the election, Trudeau had had no choice but to "get elected through the present Liberal machine".

Once Trudeau had won the nomination the rest was almost a rubber stamp process. Alan Macnaughton, the Liberal incumbent who had given up his seat for a senatorship, had left a majority in the last election of 28,973 for Trudeau. Although Trudeau's majority was less than half of that in the November 8 election, he won comfortably. His friends Pelletier and Marchand also won their seats, the former with a 7,029 majority and the latter by the surprisingly narrow margin of only 849 votes.

Nationally, the Liberal Party had been returned to a minority position, with a net increase of only two seats, but with the "three wise men" from Quebec. Marchand was immediately appointed minister of citizenship and immigration, while Trudeau had to wait until early January, 1966 before his surprise appointment – parliamentary assistant to Prime Minister Lester Pearson.

As one report noted, "Trudeau will be in a strategic position to make his influence felt. He is now very close to the decision-making centres, perhaps closer than most cabinet ministers."[5]

The election of the three roused the attention of one of Canada's foremost political journalists, Blair Fraser, early in the New Year.

"The Three do not wish to be so docile as to have no effect on Liberal policy. They are men of the Left, and they want the Liberal Party to be a party of the Left.

"The Three make no bones about their continuing sympathy with the NDP and their dislike of many aspects and individuals of the old-line Liberals. Their announced reason for joining the Liberals was that the Liberals were almost certain to form a government, whereas the NDP was by no means certain of electing even one member from Quebec."[6]

One regular contributor to Cité Libre who had won the Montreal-Dollard seat, Jean-Pierre Goyer, began mobilizing support for Trudeau in the Liberal caucus almost immediately. He re-read all of Trudeau's old contributions to Cité Libre. "I know Trudeau best by what he's written – and it's the best way to know him. He doesn't deviate from his writings. Just about everything he thinks is there."[7]

Goyer helped organize twice-weekly lectures to the caucus on problems confronting Canada, and Trudeau was frequently one of those giving the lectures. Within months the group had control of the Quebec element of the caucus and planned in detail the founding convention of the Quebec Section of the Liberal Federation of Canada in Quebec City, February 24 to 26. While many provincial Liberals had been showing an increasing sympathy for at least a special constitutional status for Quebec, the convention voted almost unanimously to keep Quebec in Canada under the present constitution.

Spring came and passed into a summer that shocked many: the provincial Liberals under Jean Lesage were beaten by a resurgent National Union Party under Daniel Johnson June 5. Less than six years after Lesage's victory had heralded the coming of the "Quiet Revolution," Duplessis' successors were back in power.

Trudeau kept his head down and began making points. One perceptive report noted in the fall that "Trudeau is now regarded as one of the most brilliant constitutional minds in Ottawa and has become one of the real philosophers of federal policy".[8]

At about the same time, another long-time Trudeau supporter, Marc Lalonde, became another of his friends at court. Lalonde had been appointed a part-time advisor to a privy council office task force on security regulations and corporate disclosures the previous winter, but was retained at the end of his contract as an advisor on federal-provincial affairs, a subject which was destined to become important.

The same month, the death knell for John Diefenbaker as party leader sounded when his nominee for the presidency of the national party association, Arthur Maloney, was narrowly defeated. On November 15, 1966 Dalton Camp won the position by a vote of 564 to 502, and it was known that Camp wanted a new national leader to replace Diefenbaker, who had then lost two elections.

But if he had lost those elections, Pearson had barely won them and some of his cabinet ministers were actively jockeying for a good position when a Liberal leadership convention was called.

Since the 1880's the Liberals had alternated English and French Canadian party leaders, and in January of 1967, Trudeau and six others began to meet to discuss separatism and a possible French Canadian to succeed Pearson. In the group were Marchand, Pelletier, Goyer, Lalonde, Maurice Sauvé, and Lamontagne.

By the end of the month Pearson admitted that Trudeau was working on constitutional problems with Lalonde and his position was again strengthened. Pearson heightened speculation about his leadership with an announcement February 5, 1967 that he favoured an open convention to choose a successor. The following month Pearson appointed Lalonde to a full time position in the privy council office as a special advisor on constitutional matters.

It seemed natural when Pearson appointed Trudeau minister of justice on April 4, but it excited much comment in the press. The Toronto Telegram's Douglas Fisher and Harry Crowe commented with much prescience that "predictions aren't worth much but we predict ... he will fascinate and bewilder those who watch our political scene more than any other politician of this generation".[9]

The next day they enthused, "So Pierre Elliot Trudeau is Canada's minister of justice. Incredible. But also wonderful." Another of the newspaper's columnists was not so enthusiastic.

"The New Democrats now have three French Canadians in the Pearson ministry. Jean Marchand, Pierre Elliott Trudeau and Jean Chretien. Not bad for a party which has so far failed to elect a single MP in Quebec under its own banner," wrote Lubor Zink.

"A few more cabinet shuffles of this kind and the NDP will form the government of this country without even trying. Prime Minister Pearson will do it for them."

Trudeau soon revealed his philosophy as minister of justice in an interview three weeks after his appointment.

"Justice should be regarded more and more as a department of planning for the society of tomorrow, not merely the government's legal advisor. It should combine the function of drafting new legislation with the disciplines of sociology and economics, so that it can provide a framework for our evolving way of life ... If possible, we have to move the framework of society slightly ahead of the times, so there is no curtailment of intellectual or physical liberty."[10]

Peter Newman, the chief of the Toronto Star's Ottawa bureau who had interviewed Trudeau, was plainly captivated.

"His intelligent, skull-formed face (which might have been carved in alabaster to commemorate some distant war of the crusades) is a pattern of tension, subtlety and audacity. He is a man who both in his physical presence and intellectual discourse manages to maintain a detached view of his environment, yet at the same time give the impression of being responsive to the play of political forces around him ... Trudeau is an agent of ferment, a critic of Canadian society, questioning its collected conventional wisdom."

On May 30, Trudeau appointed H. Carl Goldenberg as special counsel on constitutional matters, with an ex-Edmonton professor, Ivan Head, as assistant counsel. About a month later an astute political journalist, Fraser Kelly, wrote of Trudeau in a feature-length article that "some of the power bosses are already talking about him in terms of a potential leader".[11]

A week later, while in the throes of uncertainty, Canada had her one hundredth birthday at the lavish extravaganza of Expo '67. For a few weeks worries about unemployment and separatism were forgotten by the nation.

Shortly after Dominion Day Guy Favreau died and Trudeau's situation altered accordingly. Pearson had favoured Favreau as his French Canadian successor but now, as he later admitted, he looked to Trudeau. Events over the next six months would dovetail neatly to give Trudeau repeated nation-wide exposure.

On September 4, Trudeau pleaded the case for entrenching a charter of human rights in the constitution before the Canadian Bar Association. The very next day, Pearson called a constitutional conference for February, 1968, in which Trudeau would play a key, high-profile role.

While Trudeau's political fortunes had been on the rise, the Conservatives had not been idle. On September 9, after five ballots, the much-respected Robert Stanfield was elected leader, and the party gained a new lease on life.

In Quebec, the question of separatism came more sharply into focus when Trudeau's old friend, René Lévesque, openly opted for Quebec independence. As a member of the Liberals' shadow cabinet, his days were numbered. At the convention of the Liberals' Quebec wing in mid-October, Lévesque resigned from the party and, within a month, had formed a new separatist party, the Sovereignty Association Movement.

To pre-empt any possibility that the convention might take a swing toward separatism, Trudeau and his group in Ottawa made sure that Pierre Levasseur, a federalist, was elected the executive director of the party's Quebec section during the convention.

When Trudeau was not preparing his mammoth package of legislation, he worked on compiling a series of his articles and essays. These were published in the form of a collection entitled "Federalism and the French Canadians". Gerard Pelletier wrote the preface to it and said of his friend, "I have no hesitation in saying that I consider Pierre Trudeau's work to be the most serious effort to formulate a political theory for Quebec and Canada that has been attempted in the past 25 years. Whether or not his conclusions, or even the general direction of his thought, are accepted, no one can deny the intellectual integrity that characterizes these essays, the exceptional erudition on which they are based . . . it is rare to find persons in whom an entire lifetime of study and meditation has resulted in a genuine theory of politics – that is, a complete and coherent system of responses based on a clear conception of men and society."[12]

The book sold slowly at first, during October, then picked up quickly and plans were made to translate it and print it in English.

Trudeau launched his first piece of legislation, a divorce reform bill, December 4, 1967 and ten days later Pearson announced to the cabinet that he would resign. The same evening, he called Trudeau and Marchand to his residence, and told them he expected one of them to run as a leadership candidate. He wanted Trudeau, but had to include Marchand as he was his Quebec lieutenant.

Four days after that, Pearson announced there would be a leadership convention April 4 to 6, 1968 and on December 21 Trudeau grabbed the headlines when he presented his omnibus bill, which would expand the grounds for abortion and legalize homosexuality.

By now pressure had increased considerably on Trudeau and he escaped to an island in the south Pacific for a two-week vacation for rest and reflection.

He came back to find that several Liberal cabinet ministers were already campaigning hard for Pearson's mantle, and that Walter Gordon, the president of the privy council, had endorsed him as a candidate if Jean Marchand refused to run. Fisher and Crowe wrote that they believed Trudeau would be the Quebec candidate and added, "we've helped the Trudeau build-up".[13] But they then issued a warning that while most of the other candidates either had a long political record or a record of diverse achievements, Trudeau didn't. They quoted J. K. Galbraith: "if we foster great expectations, we must count on deep disillusion."

Pearson felt compelled to say that a tour of the ten provincial capitals by Trudeau had nothing to do with the leadership race, but it was obvious to others that if Trudeau did declare his candidacy, the tour would help him immensely.

After touring the maritime provinces he attended the Montreal meeting of the Quebec Liberals on January 26. As one observer noted, "most people here now take it for granted he will enter the race sometime after the constitutional conference ... Either by design or accident, events of the past few weeks, including this convention, are tailor-made for the Trudeau mystique."[14]

One of the surprises to come out of the convention, attended by about 1,000 delegates, was the resolution to abolish the Queen as Canada's head of state. A motion proposed by the Young Liberals resolved to combine the functions of the Queen and the Governor General in a president who would be elected for a five-year term by a two-thirds majority of the House of Commons and the Senate. Gerard Pelletier and another Liberal MP supported the motion and it was carried 135 to 33. Marchand abstained from the voting with Jean-Luc Pépin, the minister of energy, mines and resources, although Marchand later admitted he agreed with the motion in principle. Trudeau wasn't present for the vote, but was later quoted as saying that although he classed the monarchy "below skiing and snowshoeing" he didn't consider its abolition a priority "at this time".[15]

On the final day of the convention, Trudeau delivered a cool, rational defence of federalism to a packed hall and was rewarded with a standing ovation, three cheers and a song. He not only successfully opposed special status for Quebec, he emerged from the convention as the prime candidate for the leadership race, even though he hadn't declared himself.

In Toronto, a build-up for a Trudeau candidacy started among the academic community. A petition asking him to declare himself was circulated and soon had more than 150 signatures.

By the end of January, Zink, the Telegram's conservative columnist, was becoming increasingly concerned.

"What we are witnessing is an attempt by groups of our self-styled 'progressives', which mostly cluster along the 'avant-garde' fringes of the academic community, to create a Trudeau psychosis that would irresistibly carry the Justice Minister to victory at the Liberal leadership convention in April.

"You can't pick up a newspaper these days, or tune into any of the radio and TV news and public affairs programs, without having the alleged inevitability of Trudeau's prime ministership thrust on you.

"Though the new messiah of the 'progressive' fraternity has yet to declare his candidacy for Lester Pearson's job, the Trudeau build-up has already reached the stage where every journalist who lives in holy fear of being branded a 'reactionary' would sooner swallow his typewriter or microphone than write or say anything that could be regarded as disagreement with the tone-setting line.

"When he decided to run as a Liberal, it was known he and his like-minded friends in Quebec had formerly been at least strongly sympathetic to the NDP if, indeed, not active members.

"Is this the type of man the Liberals can entrust with the leadership of their party? And can they, without giving the electorate a say in the matter, force on the country a prime minister whose political philosophy is that of a group most Canadians consistently refuse to vote for in general elections?

"In theory – and with the help of the left-wing chorus in the mass media, perhaps even in practice – they can. But there can be little doubt that by doing so they would wreck their party."[16]

The same night that Zink's column appeared, a group of 30 Liberals met in a Toronto home to form a draft-Trudeau committee. Chairing the group were two MPs, Donald S. Macdonald from Rosedale and Robert Stanbury from York-Scarborough.

The next day Trudeau arrived back in Ottawa after the last of his provincial visits and put final touches on the preparations for the constitutional conference. But even as he was doing that, opposition started to appear to his undeclared candidacy for the leadership.

A maverick Liberal MP, Ralph Cowan, said "no man can lead me to legalizing buggery, bestiality, gross indecency or street-walking". But that comment was quickly forgotten when Trudeau and Daniel Johnson openly and bitterly clashed February 6, the second day of the constitutional conference.

Johnson called Trudeau the member from Mount Royal – a predominantly English-speaking riding – and charged that if Trudeau's ideas were taken to their logical conclusion, there would be no need for provinces.

Trudeau lashed back by calling Johnson an Irishman and angrily accused him of trying to destroy French Canadians in Ottawa.

Pearson was finally forced to step in and called a coffee break to cool the atmosphere down, but Johnson then charged that Trudeau was using the conference as a springboard toward the leadership of the Liberal Party.

Neither man had a clear upper hand in the exchanges. One report quoted a "top politician in Canada" as saying of Trudeau, "He's got a lot to learn about politics. He's very bright, but Danny was chewing him."

But other reports emphasized Trudeau's arguments that federal MPs from Quebec were the true voice of Quebec in confederation and that the concept of special status for Quebec would destroy the federal foundations of Canada.

A few days after the confrontation, Trudeau got a clear reading of how English-speaking Liberals viewed his performance when he spoke at an annual conference of the Liberal Party in Ontario in Toronto, February 9.

The headline of an article describing his reception by the Liberals told the whole story the next day: "Trudeau's Magic Stuns Liberals."

Ralph Cowan redoubled his efforts and began distributing copies of Trudeau's 1963 Cité Libre article in which he called the Liberals a "spineless herd" and Pearson the "unfrocked priest of peace". His efforts did not receive a sympathetic hearing from the press – one article about him was entitled "Cowan Starts Smear Tactics".[17]

On Thursday, February 15, Jean de Grandpré, Trudeau's old classmate from his Jean de Brébeuf days and by this time a rising star in Bell Canada, sought him out on Parliament Hill.

Trudeau had called him and asked for his advice on whether he should run for the Liberal leadership.

"I tried to dissuade him for two and a half hours," de Grandpré later recalled. The two of them paced the corridors of Parliament from the Senate to the Commons and back again.

"I said, you're too independent to operate with all the political restraints you'll have. He gave me the other side and said it couldn't be Marchand and he had to get involved, he couldn't be a quitter. He was tortured internally."

Despite de Grandpré's efforts, Trudeau announced his candidacy the next day, and became the eleventh contender for the leadership. He said he had only decided to run for certain the night before and added, "I think it started out as a huge practical joke on the Liberal Party". He also told the press he thought they "had a lot to do with it".

Reminded of some of his writings in Cité Libre that were critical of the Liberals, he said "everything I wrote I stand by". He was also questioned on an episode he had referred to in passing previously – being blacklisted by the United States. He explained that he was going to attend a commonwealth conference in Pakistan in 1956 or 1957 and had thought of returning to Canada via San Francisco and wanted to make sure he wouldn't be stopped at the port as he had heard that he had been blacklisted from entering the country.

"I presume the reasons for it to be twofold: I had been to the economic conference in Moscow in 1952, at the time Stalin was at the height of his power, and there were not many foreigners going to Russia . . . Another thing is probably that I had always received left periodicals and papers and I suspected then that there was some check on the mail, who is on the mailing list and so on. So, you know, they must have arrived at a conclusion that I was interested in . . . progressive things."

He checked with the American consulate in Montreal and yes, he was blacklisted. "How do I whiten myself?" he asked the consul. "He told me and I whitened myself."

But Lubor Zink of the Telegram, three days after Trudeau's explanation, wrote that that version gave him "some misgivings about the candidate's insistence on always telling the truth.

"The simple fact behind this fairy tale of implied witchhunting is this: On March 9, 1954, Mr. Trudeau applied for admission to the United States. He was told that due to some of the information he gave in answering the routine questionnaire, he was temporarily excluded from entry to the U.S. pending a review of that information.

"A week later, on March 16, 1954, he was sent a letter informing him that there was no objection to his intention to go to the States."

But within days, Trudeau's press conference and his candidacy were overshadowed by a parliamentary crisis that immobilized the government and the leadership race. On Wednesday, February 28, the government lost a vote on a major tax bill. The Conservatives declared that it constituted a loss of confidence in the government – and a loss of confidence usually meant an immediate election. For days the situation was uncertain, and Trudeau became involved in the government's battle to stay alive which was successful eventually. Mitchell Sharp had been finance minister and deputy prime minister, and was the candidate to suffer most from the crisis. While Pearson had been away on vaction, he had been charged with handling the government's business, and had bungled it.

With the crisis over, however, Trudeau's campaign continued. Growing crowds were increasingly enthusiastic over his give-and-take style of speaking. It was becoming clear that instead of a dark-horse candidate, he would be a leading contender in the race. But opposition was mounting quietly, in part because of his background. He fuelled the fires of his opposition with statements like the one he made in London, Ontario on March 8.

He was asked if he would adopt socialist policies if he were prime minister and replied:

"Any policy which is good in a given situation, which can solve a problem, without destroying the basic beliefs I have in freedom and democracy, I would not hesitate to follow. I'm not a believer in doctrines."

A political observer wrote "in 1965 the Liberal Party was being threatened by the New Democratic Party. So, as it has done so often in the past, it reached out and grabbed three of the more attractive socialists in the land – Trudeau, Manpower Minister Jean Marchand and Gerard Pelletier.

"Now these men seem to be in a position to make a real bid to take over the party, or at least exert tremendous influence on it – all in less than three years."[18]

Then in early March, the English language edition of "Federalism and the French Canadians" was published with an introduction by John Saywell, the Dean of Arts and Sciences of York University in Toronto, and it sold like hot cakes.

Saywell made no bones about what he thought Trudeau's beliefs were. He wrote, "To many people, Pierre Elliott Trudeau has seemed enigmatic and paradoxical: a man of substantial wealth, yet a democratic socialist; an advocate of extensive state power who denies that anyone knows better than he what is good for him . . . "[19]

Trudeau started to mention some of the changes he would like to see take place if he were elected prime minister. He wanted to recognize mainland China and reform parliament.

Canada needed "the kind of adaptability that enables us to change and change quickly," he said and that could only happen when parliament had a new set of rules. He said he didn't see his lack of experience as a drawback, because frequently knowledge of the rules resulted in someone taking ten days to solve a problem that should have been solved in a matter of hours.

He said that Canada should withdraw from NATO and concentrate on NORAD, although he wanted Canada to retain its diplomatic influence within the alliance.

Trudeau received some support for his candidacy from an

unlikely source – the head of the separatist RIN, Pierre Bour-gault. He believed that if Trudeau became prime minister it would hasten the independence of Quebec. "He's the best candidate we could hope for."

In the few days before the leadership convention, Trudeau's campaign seemed to gather a momentum that would be impossible to stop. Mitchell Sharp dropped out of the race and declared for Trudeau, and soon other MPs followed suit. Premier Joey Smallwood said he would deliver all 84 Newfoundland delegates to Trudeau, though it appeared that almost half of them might vote differently.

At last April 6 arrived and 2400 delegates, the media and party officials packed into the steamy Ottawa Civic Centre to start balloting.

Three hundred of those delegates had received a small pamphlet which must have shocked some of them entitled "MEMO-RANDUM: Trudeau, a Potential Canadian Castro". The author of the pamphlet was none other than Igor Gouzenko, the defector from the Soviet Embassy in Ottawa who had shaken the country by exposing an extensive spy ring in 1945.

"Because Canadian and U.S. press, radio and television largely ignored the past activities and writings of Trudeau, the public is not aware of a real possibility that on the 6th of April, 1968, the next Prime Minister of Canada might be a self-admitted radical socialist, and Canada might with ever increasing pace turn into a second Cuba. The situation is already pregnant with a multiple threat to Canadian freedom."

In the 13-page memorandum Gouzenko outlined some of Trudeau's past activities and writings and linked him tenuously, and sometimes incorrectly, to some dubious figures. He reminded the delegates they would not just be electing a new party leader, but a new prime minister.

"When you are going to vote the fate of our country will be in your hands. Think a million times – for each man, woman and child in Canada – before you cast your ballot."

In the first ballot Trudeau received 752 votes, a little less than one third of the total, but in a field of eight effective contenders, it gave him a commanding lead. By the third ballot, Robert Winters, who represented the right wing of the party and balanced budgets, was the sole contender who could beat him, but the next ballot gave the leadership to Trudeau by a 250 vote margin.

Thirty months after joining the Liberal Party and winning his first election, Pierre Elliott Trudeau was prime minister.

FOOTNOTES CHAPTER 11

1. This account of the press conference and the events immediately leading up to it are taken from Martin Sullivan, "Mandate '68," Doubleday Canada Limited, Toronto, 1968, pp 93-97.
2. From an interview with the author, July 26, 1977.
3. Cité Libre, October, 1965.
4. Le Devoir, October 19, 1965.
5. Toronto Star, January 22, 1966.
6. Maclean's Magazine, January 22, 1966.
7. Sullivan, op cit, p. 122.
8. Montreal Gazette, November 9, 1966.
9. Toronto Telegram, April 5, 1967.
10. Toronto Star, April 25, 1967.
11. Toronto Telegram, June 24, 1967.
12. Pierre Elliott Trudeau, "Federalism and the French Canadians," Macmillan of Canada, Toronto, 1968, p. xvi.
13. Toronto Telegram, January 19, 1968.
14. Toronto Telegram, January 27, 1968.
15. Toronto Telegram, January 27, 1968.
16. Toronto Telegram, January 31, 1968.
17. Toronto Telegram, February 15, 1968.
18. Toronto Telegram, March 9, 1968.
19. Trudeau, op cit, p. vii.

12

Ten Years Later

Trudeau's decade of power as prime minister has passed astonishingly quickly.

In it, he has given innumerable press conferences, read hundreds of speeches and travelled tens of thousands of miles for scores of meetings.

He presides over a record 34-member cabinet and is responsible indirectly for legions of civil servants and consultants.

In this crowded welter of activity the image of Trudeau that emerges is blurred and sometimes confusing, in sharp contrast to the clarity of his image before he entered federal politics.

To bring Prime Minister Trudeau into sharp focus, a critical question has to be answered.

Does Prime Minister Trudeau of 1978 hold the same beliefs as Pierre Elliott Trudeau of 1950, 1960 or 1965?

Trudeau's oldest, closest friend is Gerard Pelletier. Last fall he told me "I know Trudeau as well as I can know any man.

"He has devoted his whole thinking since the age of 14 toward politics and toward power and the use of it. He has a coherent, well structured view of what politics is all about. He knows where he is going and why."

Trudeau's basic ideas are "definitely" the same as ever, he said. Ten years before this interview, Pelletier had made a similar statement in his preface to the collection of Trudeau's essays entitled "Federalism and the French Canadians".

"The essays that follow were written over a number of years,"

Pelletier then wrote. "This makes it all the more admirable that they complement each other so well and are moulded by the internal logic of an unwavering line of thought into a solid, coherent whole."

In his introduction to the English edition of the same collection, Professor John Saywell noted the same characteristic.

"Consistency is, in fact, the most remarkable quality of Mr. Trudeau's thoughts and actions over the past two decades."

Jean-Pierre Goyer, whom Trudeau met and befriended 20 years ago during the Quebec university students' strike, came to the same conclusion in 1968.

"I know Pierre best by what he's written – and it's the best way to know him. He doesn't deviate from his writings. Just about everything he thinks is there."

Jean-Louis Gagnon, another old friend whom Trudeau appointed head of Information Canada when it was created, said last summer "Trudeau didn't change his ideas fundamentally from the early fifties to the time he entered the Liberal Party". In the early fifties, Gagnon termed Trudeau a "Fabian socialist".

In fact, when Trudeau issued a prepared statement with Pelletier shortly after joining the Liberal Party in September, 1965, he made it quite clear he held the same beliefs as before.

"The undersigned are still following the same goals, they are continuing to adhere to the same political ideologies that they have for a long time set forth in Cité Libre . . .

"We don't repudiate any of our convictions. We have only resolved to pursue elsewhere and in other ways, the intellectual and social struggle which has always claimed us."

While still justice minister, Trudeau was taunted with some of his former writings. He responded by saying "Everything I wrote I stand by".

Three years later, while defending a political decision, he said "I acted on the information I have been accumulating since I was three years old".

But what information, what ideas, have formed the basis for Trudeau's actions?

He himself has pinpointed three main sources for his ideas.

In 1971, Trudeau said "In my youth the people who influenced me the most were the Christian existentialists like Mounier ... "

In his last, key editorial before his death, Emmanuel Mounier wrote in his review Esprit: The proletariat "must be allowed to continue the positive work of the communist party while eliminating all the poisons which are mixed therein. Such is one of our principal tasks for tomorrow.

"We will emphasize that as much as possible in our review, and our wish is that one day we can work together in such a task with a purified communism."

In 1966, Trudeau said he found Professor Harold Laski of the London School of Economics "the most stimulating and powerful influence" he had encountered.

Laski's single most important book, "A Grammar of Politics," which Trudeau studied, laid out these central principles:

"The necessarily federal character of society; the incompatibility of the sovereign state with that economic world order so painfully struggling to be born; the antithesis between individual property rights in the essential means of production and the fulfilment of the democratic idea; the thesis that liberty is a concept devoid of real meaning except in the context of equality ...

"There cannot, in a word, be democracy unless there is socialism ... "

In 1976, Trudeau said that "In terms of economics, you know, I spent two years studying with Schumpeter and two years studying with Leontief and if you want to know who is permeating my economic thinking you'd do better to think in terms of Leontief and Schumpeter".

Schumpeter, Trudeau's Harvard professor, wrote as his major work, "Capitalism, Socialism and Democracy".

In it, Schumpeter wrote, "I have tried to show that a socialist form of society will inevitably emerge from an equally inevitable decomposition of capitalist society."

So it may be reasonably said that Trudeau's ideas, drawn from the writings of Schumpeter, Laski and Mounier, have remained basically the same for the past 30 years.

Let's quickly review his past writings, then, compare them with his more recent statements, and see how they might affect Canadians.

On Democracy and Freedom

1958: "What regime, or what system, gives the maximum guarantee against oppression?

"A possible reply here would be that it is conceivable that a benevolent despot might rule wisely, establish a just order for all his subjects, and leave them enough freedom of expression. Would such a regime not be based on the consent of the people?

"Yes, this is conceivable. But such consent clearly could not be taken for granted. A mechanism would have to be provided to allow the people to express their opinions freely on the excellence of the despot. There would also have to be some device to ensure that the despot would abdicate if opinion went against him. And finally a means would have to be invented to designate, peacefully, a successor whom the people would agree to obey. But clearly such a regime would no longer be called a despotism; it would have borrowed the actual mechanism of democracy.

"And it must be recognized that democracy is the form of government we are looking for.

"I as well, I believe in the necessity of state control to maximize the liberty and welfare of all, and to permit everyone to realize himself fully. But I would prefer to renounce socialism rather than admit that one should construct it on undemocratic foundations: Russia has shown us that that is the way of totalitarianism."

"I'm personally convinced that with the upheavals promised by automation, cybernetics and thermo-nuclear energy, liberal democracy will not long be able to satisfy our growing demands for justice and liberty, and that it should evolve toward a form of social democracy. But I am willing to help with the establishment of a liberal democracy precisely because I believe the other will follow afterwards. A liberal democrat will doubtless be convinced otherwise; but what does that matter?"

1961: "I should like to see socialists feeling free to espouse whatever political trends or to use whatever constitutional tools happen to fit each particular problem at each particular time . . .

"In a non-revolutionary society and in non-revolutionary times . . . democratic reformers must proceed step by step, convincing little bands of intellectuals here, rallying sections of the working class there, and appealing to the underprivileged in the next place. The drive toward power must begin with the establishment of bridgeheads, since at the outset it is obviously easier to convert specific groups or localities than to win over an absolute majority of the whole nation.

"Since the future of Canadian federalism lies clearly in the direction of co-operation, the wise socialist will turn his thoughts in that direction, keeping in mind the importance of establishing buffer zones of joint sovereignty and co-operative zones of joint administration between the two levels of government."

1962: "If our intellectuals had read a little Marx, Lenin and Mao Tse-tung, they would know that true revolutionaries are ready to accept a tactical compromise if necessary to allow a still-young left to come into the world."

1964: "For humanity, progress is the slow journey toward personal freedom. . . . Certainly there are historical cases in which personal freedom has scarcely been protected at all by established institutions; it has been possible, then, for a genuine revolutionary to stress collective freedom as a preliminary to personal freedom: Castro, Ben Bella, Lenin . . .

"But when personal freedom exists, it would be inconceivable that a revolutionary should destroy it in the name of some collective ideology. For the very purpose of a collective system is better to ensure personal freedom."

1977: "Some legitimate and even convincing cases have been made that in certain countries at certain times that [one-party democracy] is a good form of democracy. I wouldn't be prepared to think I would be successful in arguing that for Canada at the present time, but such times might come, who knows?"

On the Free Market System and Private Property

1956: "In the scheme of production, private initiative and property, collective initiative and co-operative property, public initiative and nationalization, are only *means* in the service of human and economic objectives...

"It's impossible to predict which ideal economic structures must be put in place... Meanwhile, in our highly industrialized societies, private initiative left to itself can't guarantee common prosperity. That must be assured through planning."

"Clearly, when the revolution produced by automation, cybernetics, and nuclear energy has completely altered the foundations of the present regime of property and authority; when a certain amount of state planning has become an absolute necessity for controlling the chaotic conditions of the period of transition and when nationalization of the principal means of production has become an established fact, there will still be clerics around to proclaim, with an old text of Pius XI in hand, that the social doctrine of the Church has never ceased to be avantgarde.

"Let us bear clearly in mind that there is no question here of proclaiming a new regime of industrial liberty, nor of advocating socialism, still less of sketching an economic theory of plenty for all. It is simply a matter of prosaically applying the lessons of the last fifty years to the present."

1957: "You can see that a country under the thumb of economic domination can only get out from under it if it practises planning. For that, Canadian nationalism would have to become economically interventionist, and politicians would have to think more about the common good than their election warchest.

"But that's probably asking too much. Canadians want an economic regime that has all the advantages of being controlled; but they want to get them without a controlled economy . . . "

1958: "As far as I go, it seems evident to me that the regime of free enterprise has shown itself incapable of adequately resolving problems posed in education, health, housing, full employment etc. That's why I'm personally convinced that with the upheavals promised by automation, cybernetics and thermo-nuclear energy, liberal democracy will not long be able to satisfy our growing demands for justice and liberty, and that it should evolve toward a form of social democracy."

1961: "The nationalization of the instruments of production is now being considered less as an end than as a means, and one that might in many cases be replaced by more flexible processes of economic control and redistribution.

"The erroneous, liberal idea of property helped to emancipate the bourgeoisie but is now hampering the march toward economic democracy."

1975: "We haven't been able to make it work, the free market system . . . the government is going to have to take a larger role in running institutions . . . It means there is going to be not less authority in our lives but perhaps more . . . "

1976: "We haven't been able to make even a modified free market system work in Canada to prevent the kinds of problems we are now experiencing . . . "

1978: "Just two years ago I talked about that type of [economic] challenge and I dared to mention the word new society, I think, and everybody in the country who was on a corporate board fell off his chair. Now after visiting the premiers I've been talking in terms of new methods of economic policy setting and new economic directions and people are now beginning to see that this is necessary . . . Our economic crisis is forcing us into making the kind of choices which I think will be great for the future of the country."

On Entering the Liberal Party

1956: Citizens "refuse to believe that there's only one way of getting into politics: by entering one of the old parties and 'changing it from the inside'. By believing this myth, successive generations have seen their energy and political sincerity annihilated. We find it's essential to look elsewhere in the future."

1958: "One can say . . . that a prime minister 'gives himself' to his country or province, in the sense that the time he devotes to the administration of public business is out of proportion to the indemnity he receives from the public treasury.

"But it does not necessarily follow that such a gift is always to the advantage of the recipients: there are some gifts one would do well not to accept, as the Trojans learned to their cost some years ago!"

1965: "I think it's only normal, after spending 15 years as a critic in the role of a critic, after telling others what to do, to try and get out and do it myself."

"It must never be forgotten that in the democracies that we know, the political party isn't an end but a means, not a goal, but an instrument. He who enters a political party, then, is choosing a tool. . . .

"We don't repudiate any of our convictions. We have only resolved to pursue elsewhere and in other ways, the intellectual and social struggle which has always claimed us."

1968: Question: "I was wondering if you could explain to us why you have changed your political philosophy from the times you were an editor of Cité Libre and a severe critic of the Liberal Party to your present philosophy which allows you to be leader of the Liberal Party of Canada and Prime Minister?"

Trudeau: "There's a mistake here. Just because the Liberal Party has changed its philosophy you shouldn't assume that I've changed mine. . . . No party, no matter how venerable and old and structured and bossed by machines and imbued in history, and controlled by strongmen, no party can really escape the control of a group of people who want to get in there and decide to control it. Which we did."

On Election Platforms

1964: "Public figures, federal and provincial, do not provide the people with a clear idea of the direction in which they want the country to go . . . our political leaders want to be all things to all men. They propose goals so vague and incoherent that the voters can never be sure of the relationship between what is said today and done tomorrow."

1973: "Any system of prices and incomes controls has thus far been rejected as ineffective in coping with inflation."

1974: "One thing about the [wage and price] freeze is clear. We can't freeze the prices on goods coming into Canada . . . So while your wages are frozen, those prices will be going up. Wage and price freezes have already been tried in the United States and Great Britain. It didn't work there. And they won't work here."

1975: "Tomorrow, the government of Canada will ask parliament for the authority to impose severe restraints upon rising prices and incomes."

1978: "I believe in the parliamentary system. I believe that political parties should stand for something clearly, they should present it and they should stand or fall on the choice of the electorate on whether they should proceed or not."

On the Queen, Parliament and the Opposition

1968: At a convention, the Quebec Liberals passed a resolution to abolish the monarchy. It proposed the duties of the Queen and the Governor General be combined in a president who would be elected for five years by a two-thirds majority of the House of Commons and the Senate. Pelletier voted for the resolution, while Marchand abstained, saying that although he agreed with it in principle, it was not the time to take a firm stand.

Trudeau was absent for the vote, although he was later quoted as saying that he classed the Queen "below skiing and snowshoeing". He added that he didn't consider abolishing the monarchy a priority "at this time".

1977: After a request by the Canadian government, Trudeau announced that the Queen had agreed to give up virtually all her remaining powers. The Governor General assumed the powers to accredit and recall Canadian diplomats, authorize declarations of war, and sign peace treaties.

The length of the Queen's visit to Canada during her jubilee year was cut in half and Canada's "definitive" stamp was changed to show the Parliament buildings instead of her portrait.

1958: "I choke with indignation at the humiliations inflicted on that Opposition. The point is that in a parliamentary democracy the Opposition is the last and most important bulwark against arbitrary tyranny; through it the people reserve the right to criticize from moment to moment the way they are governed — through it they nip legislative and administrative abuses in the bud."

1964: "The Opposition is supposed to force the Government to define their policies and to furnish the public with all relevant information. The Opposition is supposed to proclaim the true problems of the people, for it is the conscience of the Government.

"At the same time, however, the present state of our parliamentary mechanism is such that the Opposition, even when it is vigilant, is virtually helpless in the face of the resources available to the Government. The system must be reformed to give the Opposition at state expense the tools which are necessary for it to fulfil its important and true role."

1968: "It is complete nonsense to have 29 ministers hanging around for one and a half or two hours every day just in case some guy in the Opposition thinks up a question."

The government under Trudeau introduced a parliamentary reform package. One reform set a rotation schedule for ministers, so that they wouldn't have to be in the House every day. Another, which the government eventually withdrew after a storm of opposition both in and out of Parliament, provided for setting a limit on debate before it started. The rule would have allowed the government to set the limit itself. Trudeau claimed the latter rule had only been inserted to allow the others to pass, once it had been withdrawn.

"We pulled the ground out from under them, and Parliament has a completely new set of rules . . .

"To get the job done requires having the government run in the right way. And that is why we are re-shaping our institutions and spending so much time on it in the early months of this government. I have the feeling of . . . a mechanic who's re-tuning a car or something and getting the thing ready to go."

1969: "If I were to summarize my feelings on my first year in office, I would say it has been a year in which I have had the satisfaction of seeing the Government gradually take control of the mechanism of politics. We have instituted reforms in Parliament, making it more efficient under the new rules . . . Beyond that, we have reorganized the machinery of government in general."

He then re-introduced the rule which had been so strongly rejected six months before, and with the sheer weight of numbers, imposed closure on the debate and passed it.

"When they (the Opposition) get home, when they get out of Parliament, when they are 50 yards from Parliament Hill, they are no longer Honourable Members – they are just nobodies.

"I think we should encourage the Opposition to leave. Every time they do, the I.Q. of the House rises considerably."

1971: "Fuck-off." [Trudeau said it twice to the Opposition, mouthing the words silently, so that the Hansard reporters couldn't record it.]

On Foreign Policy and Defence

1951: "The United States can't forgive the Chinese people for chasing out the Kuomintang [Chiang Kai-shek's forces] whose shameful corruption wasn't at all incompatible with international high finance . . . It's impossible to believe that the lightning war unleashed by the North Koreans and the subsequent reunification of the whole of Korea under a government, even communist, atheist or totalitarian, would have been able to produce as many collective injustices . . . as those which resulted from the military intervention by the United Nations."

1954: "Perhaps the world will one day understand that it would be better to fill the void in global demand by distributing purchasing power to starving countries rather than make war on them."

1956: "Whatever the motives are that lead men to group themselves into distinct societies, the ultimate allegiance of each is to the human race. Men of all countries are dependent upon each other and in time of need they should help out each other with brotherly aid."

1968: "We are hoping that Europe – and the world – will evolve beyond this political partition of spheres of influence, and our foreign-policy review is an attempt to go beyond that." [Trudeau made this statement shortly after the Soviet invasion of

Czechoslovakia. He had also said he still thought détente was possible.]

1968: "Canada is in the extraordinarily fortunate position of not having to defend itself because we know darn well that the United States will defend us. They won't let a hostile nation take over Canada to wage war on the United States.

"So, in a sense, we are much freer than other nations, and I believe we should use this freedom to explore . . . ways in which middle-sized nations can move the world toward peace, in a way in which many European countries cannot."

1969: Canada is concluding its "first methodical and total review of our foreign policy and our defence policy since the end of World War II. We have gone back to first principles in doing so, and we are questioning the continuing validity of many assumptions."

"I am not interested in protecting a few Canadian cities if this means we will be consenting to a kind of policy which we think is dangerous to the world."

1972: "We started from the proposition that our foreign policy should try and abstract itself from former prejudices, those mainly of the cold war."

1974: "We are now re-orienting our foreign policy, our trade policy, and indeed our military policy in a way which is breaking the pattern of the past 100 years."

1961: "The accredited anti-communists, of course, will go on believing for the next 50 years that the Chinese are on the verge of rising against their Communist government, just as some people have believed the same of the U.S.S.R. for 44 years. China's methods are going to be imitated by the two-thirds of the human race that goes to bed hungry every night. And the moral indignation of the West will be powerless to stop it."

When visiting China, Trudeau met Rewi Alley, a western communist who had lived in China for many years.

1971: When Trudeau visited the People's Republic of China he invited Alley to a state banquet as his guest. Alley recalls, "Mr. Trudeau took me over to his table and sat me down by Premier Chou En-lai, so that I talked for a while with him and Vice-Premier Teng Shao-ping, before returning to my place, and after meeting Mrs. Trudeau. Mr. Trudeau is obviously a leader of ability, charm and sincerity, with considerable strength of character. I think he appreciates today's China, and is keen to better Canadian Chinese relations, a very important thing in today's world."

1952: "I still believe that from the material point of view your system can be excellent for countries such as yours ... [U.S.S.R.] and I add that in your country I never saw opulence displayed which was an insult to a great many people like I have often seen in countries on the other side of the Iron Curtain.

"If you are really working for the happiness of the Russian people, and not Russian influence, it seems to me that you've got to be a little more Trotskyite, a little more Titoist.

"In every country, always be justice's agent of ferment, bring the Left together, and rise up against exploitation of man by man. But wouldn't you have to stop referring everywhere to Mister Stalin and to the glorious example of the U.S.S.R.? Only then would all the forces of the Left be able to rally together and strengthen bonds of friendship between all progressive countries.

"You would thus form a true Popular Front against reactionary forces that would know no boundaries.

"They [Russians] are determined to be strong whatever price they have to pay. That's why western politicians make me laugh when they depict Russians as a people who only live in the hope of being free of the Stalinist yoke. They won't commit this spiritual sin. On the contrary, the more they feel their country is menaced from the outside, the more they will rally around their leaders, hardening themselves into rocklike resolve."

1971: In Kiev, U.S.S.R.: "Those of your countrymen now in Canada, Mr. Chairman, though many thousands of miles away from the Ukraine, find themselves living within a constitutional framework with a formal structure similar to that in the Soviet Union. Each of our countries has chosen a federal system of government . . . its very complexity is its strength, for it permits a necessary degree of flexibility.

"We have a great deal to learn from the Soviet Union . . . a country from which we have a great deal to benefit."

Canada was befriending Russia to counter the U.S. threat "to our identity from the cultural, economic and perhaps even military point of view."

"I do not wish to leave the impression that Canada and the Soviet Union have no differences . . . They relate to deep-seated concerns springing from historic, geographic, ideological, economic, social and military factors. Nevertheless, as governments, many of our objectives are similar. We seek for our peoples a world without war, a world in which governments are at the service of man – to raise the standard of living, to eliminate disease and want, to attempt to make life a happier experience."

1977: Vladimir Bukovsky, a noted Russian dissident, said "I was in prison when Mr. Trudeau arrived in Moscow. He declared that we would like to have an exchange of experience – to use Soviet experience of development of northern territories. It was awful for us, for everybody in the Soviet Union. Everybody knew quite well how many millions of prisoners perished when developing those territories. It was awful . . . "

1964: "Certainly there are historical cases in which personal freedom has scarcely been protected at all by established institutions; it has been possible, then, for a genuine revolutionary to stress collective freedom as a preliminary to personal freedom: Castro, Ben Bella, Lenin . . . The very purpose of a collective system is better to ensure personal freedom."

1969: Trudeau was asked, "What society would you choose to make Canada? Socialist or capitalist?" Trudeau replied:

"Labour party socialist – or Cuban socialism or Chinese socialism – socialism from each according to his means."

1976: Cuban planes supplying the invasion force in Angola re-
fuel twice at Gander, Newfoundland, less than two weeks before
Trudeau is scheduled to leave for Cuba on a state visit.

In Cienfuegos, Cuba, a coastal city used as a Soviet naval port
Trudeau said, "Viva el Prime Ministro Commandante Fidel Castro!"

After his trip, it was announced that Canada had given four
million dollars to Cuba, and loaned another $10 million in a
three per cent loan to be repaid over 30 years, with repayment
starting in 1982.

1942: Trudeau, Robert and others try to smash the Gazette's
windows during a violent anti-conscription rally in Montreal.

He mocks the government in saying to students: "You were
rebels during the plebiscite. Young men, this can't go on. I will
even add that it has got to stop . . . I would give my life if that
would aid the sublime cause of the United Nations [the allies] –
yes! I would give my life to writing."

At a pro-Drapeau election meeting: "The General is campaigning in his uniform. In a democracy, I was taught, you
present yourself as a citizen, and not as the representative of a
military clique . . . using reflected glory."

1952: "Unhappily the revolution hadn't destroyed the old Russian mania for uniforms."

1968: Trudeau pledges, if elected, to withdraw militarily from
the North Atlantic Treaty Organization.

1969: "The Canadian government intends, in consultation with
Canada's allies, to take early steps to bring about a planned and
phased reduction in the size of the Canadian forces in Europe."
Shortly afterwards, in the face of cabinet and NATO protests,

the size of Canada's NATO contingent in Europe was halved and its nuclear role scrapped.

1975: Canada's defence outlay was 1.8 per cent of the Gross National Product – the lowest, after Luxembourg, among NATO powers. The latter quickly made it clear that any contractual link between the European Economic Community and Canada would partially hinge on its NATO contribution.

Jacques Dextraze, the Canadian Chief of Defence Staff and the president of the NATO military committee, spoke of "Détente in Perspective".

"Russia is the focus of an international expansionistic ideology, and ... openly, even proudly, proclaims its goal of world domination."

The huge Soviet military build-up "must in a period of détente be considered as a major destablizing factor and thus offensive in nature as it can be taken as an indication of intent."

He quoted Soviet Foreign Minister Andrei Gromyko as saying, "The forces of Peace and Progress [Warsaw Pact countries] have a visibly increased preponderance and may be in a position to lay down the direction of international politics."

"That is their interpretation of 'détente', their interpretation of the 'spirit of Helsinki,'" Dextraze continued.

" ... No other aims of our society are achievable if we fail to maintain the security of the territory and the resources of ourselves and of our friends.

" ... We must arrest the trend toward declining military strength in the West ... the liberty and freedom which we enjoy today have been dearly paid for in lives, unhappiness and money. Our way of life deserves to be protected for our children."

On the Economy

1956: "A human economy should abolish the exploitation of man by man and share production increases and leisure equally among citizens.

"This result will be attained by . . . the most equal distribution possible of the fruits and burdens of economic activity among all members collectively."

"The common good would doubtless have been better served if our [nationalist Quebec] researchers had studied the unequal distribution of our provincial wealth less from the ethnic point of view and more from the point of view of social classes and the inequities inherent in economic liberalism. To do so, however, they would have had to attack the economic dictatorship with more vigour and to devote to real reforms of structure (teaching, nationalization, planned economy etc.) some of the energy that was lavished on" economic nationalism.

1968: "Without a united country no economic progress is possible: and if the country is not surging ahead economically, it is likely to fall apart."

1976: In the period from October, 1970, to October 1976, inflation was 55.3 per cent. The money supply grew by 100.2 per cent: the economy grew by 31.7 per cent.

1977: The federal department of consumer and corporate affairs reported there were 12,224 personal and corporate bankruptcies in the first nine months of the year, a 25 per cent increase over the previous year.

In a continuing decline of the Canadian dollar's purchasing power, what could be bought for one dollar in 1971 cost $1.66 in 1977.

The inflation rate in December, on an annual rate, was 9.1 per cent.

1978: The seasonally adjusted unemployment rate was 8.5 per cent at the beginning of the year, meaning more than 1,000,000

Canadians were out of work, the worst rate since the Great Depression.

"I think the experience of any government is that it doesn't get re-elected on its record. I think our record ... is pretty darn good. The average income of Canadians has gone up by some 75 per cent in the nine years that I've been prime minister. The real standard of living has more than doubled in the past 20 years and in the last 10 it has gone up by something like 50 per cent."

On the Growth of Government

1950: "Nowhere does power not tend to grow; it's a universal law, and why should Ottawa be the exception? ... In these days, fiscal and economic theory both support the necessity of centralization ... all the ideological thrusts are for centralization."

1954: "Since neither individuals themselves, nor the economic system by itself, can remedy the economic fluctuations, we're forced – whether we like it or not – to turn to the State. How can it guarantee that distributed purchasing power will transform itself completely into effective demand for produced goods?
"The most obvious solution would be to redistribute income equally among social classes, so that the poor would have more to spend, and the rich less to save."

How could a weakened economy be stimulated?
"The answer is quite simple: the State will have budgetary deficits and finance itself through loans ... in practice, that will be done through the intermediary of the Bank of Canada which will open a credit account in the name of the government in return for loan certificates. (If the bank doesn't have enough currency in circulation, it could always print some without any inconvenience.)
"That will evidently scandalize those orthodox thinkers who

212

deem intolerable a government which deliberately puts itself in debt. But if you want to smooth out economic cycles, you must distinguish between national accounting and that of a grocery store, and understand that a country isn't ruined merely because it has lent itself a lot of money."

"To control a bureaucratic invasion, administration has to be decentralized and the role of the parliamentary committees accentuated. To prevent political equality being rendered inoperable by the sole fact of economic inequality, social legislation has to be widened.

"If citizens lose, for one moment, the control of their governmental machines, or if they let events pass them by, they will be swiftly engulfed by storms of despotism and anarchy."

1958: "We are going to be governed whether we like it or not . . . we must therefore concern ourselves with politics, as Pascal said, to mitigate, as far as possible, the damage done by the madness of our rulers."

1964: In a time of high unemployment, it is "inconceivable that politicians should continue to dread budgetary deficits and that, even when resorting to them, they should continue to pay homage to the sacred cow of a balanced budget.

"The present distribution of wealth and income among the various social groups and diverse regions of Canada is plainly unacceptable."

In 1965, when Trudeau joined the Liberal Party, the federal budget was $9.4 billion. For 1977-78, the budget is $44.5 billion, with a deficit of $8.8 billion. The cost of servicing the interest on that deficit alone is about $2 billion.

From 1968 to 1977, the number of federal civil servants and government employees grew from 375,417 to 499,666. The cost of operating the prime minister's office rose from $767,000 in 1968-69 to $2.5 million in 1977-78.

In December, 1977, the chairman of the parliamentary committee on public accounts reported that the government owns wholly or partly, 380 corporations, not 360 as the government had previously reported. The government was involved in everything from airlines and railways to farming, lotteries, motels, soft drinks, oil and mines.

In his report on the 1976-77 fiscal year, Auditor-General J. J. Macdonell said "In the majority of crown corporations audited ... financial management and control is weak and ineffective."

1978: Allen T. Lambert, head of the royal commission inquiring into the government's financial management and the accountability of the bureaucracy, reported "The old axiom that 'if something can go wrong, it will', applies with special force to governments grown as large and unwieldy as the government of Canada".

On the New Canada

1945: On Trudeau's dormitory door at Harvard: "Pierre Elliott Trudeau: Citizen of the World."

1956: The 1949 Asbestos strike "occurred at a time when we were witnessing the passing of a world, precisely at a moment when our social framework – the worm-eaten remnants of a bygone age – was ready to come apart."

Hopefully, nationalists "will one day come to realize that they will only be able to make the transition from the past to the future by means of social radicalism.

"We no longer live in a static world: we must go forward with the caravan of humanity or perish in the desert of time past. The current developments in technology and politics herald a future social and industrial revolution in comparison with which the previous one will seem but child's play."

1961: "The erroneous, liberal idea of property helped to emancipate the bourgeoisie but is now hampering the march toward economic democracy.

"Investment planning and resource development, for instance, both become in the last analysis matters for political decision ... Economic planning must eventually be reduced to political planning.

"In the debate which opposes centralization to autonomy, socialists should be as detached and pragmatic as they hope to become in the debate over public versus private ownership; those are all means, and not ends, and they must be chosen according to their usefulness in each specific case."

1962: "The nation, is, in fact, the guardian of certain very positive qualities ... They belong to a transitional period in world history ... The nation of French Canadians will some day fade from view, and ... Canada itself will undoubtedly not exist forever."

"Canada could become the envied seat of a form of federalism that belongs to tomorrow's world ... Canadian federalism is an experiment of major proportions; it could become a brilliant prototype for the moulding of tomorrow's civilization."

1964: "In the advanced societies ... where the road to progress lies in the direction of international integration, nationalism will have to be discarded as a rustic and clumsy tool."

"The most valid trends today are toward more enlightened humanism, toward various forms of political, social and economic universalism. Canada is a reproduction on a smaller and simpler scale of this universal phenomenon. ... If Canadians cannot make a success of a country such as theirs, how can they contribute in any way to the elaboration of humanism, to the formulation of the international political structures of tomorrow? To confess one's inability to make Canadian Confederation work is, at this stage of history, to admit one's unworthiness to contribute to the universal order.

"If this country is to work, federalism must be preserved and refined at all costs."

215

1967: "Justice should be regarded more and more as a department of planning for the society of tomorrow, not merely as the government's legal advisor. It should combine the function of drafting new legislation with the disciplines of sociology and economics, so that it can provide a framework for our evolving way of life . . . "

"If possible, we have to move the framework of society slightly ahead of the times, so there is no curtailment of intellectual or physical liberty."

1968: "Any policy which is good in a given situation, which can solve a problem, without destroying the basic beliefs I have in freedom and democracy, I would not hesitate to follow. I'm not a believer in doctrines."

Pierre Bourgault, head of the separatist RIN said he wanted Trudeau elected prime minister as that would hasten the independence of Quebec. "He's the best candidate we could hope for."

1977: Pierre Bourgault: "Rigid people who simplify problems — like Trudeau — are very easy to handle. It's quite easy to fight Mr. Trudeau. You just have to confront him. He has a very French mind — everything must be logical, but life and politics are not like that. It has nothing to do with real life. It's a vice for him. He exists only on the strength of his adversaries. If we didn't exist, he wouldn't be in power. I never understood why English-speaking people couldn't understand that. Confrontation had to come, but Trudeau aggravated it."

1968: "Canada must be progressive . . . The government has to orient the country to progress, economic and social progress, and make Canadian society a just society."

1969: "Federalism has its advantages, but it also has its costs, as does everything in life . . . And it sometimes does mean that we have to change the constitution to keep it up-to-date, to give the federal and provincial governments the new roles which are called for in a new society."

The following exchange between a group of students and Trudeau took place in England:

Q: "What society would you choose to make Canada? Socialist or capitalist?"

A: "Labour Party socialist – or Cuban socialism or Chinese socialism – socialism from each according to his means."

Q: "From each according to his ability, to each according to his needs? Would you support that?"

A: "Yes, in theory, but not entirely in practice. I think in history there have been some small communities who have done that, and I support this and admire it. I do not think it is workable under present circumstances.

"There is still a lot of hate and violence and injustice and inequity and racial discrimination which we shall have to overcome before ever reaching such a state. But if you ask me if it is an ideal, a beacon, something which the world should have, yes, I think it is."

"By the time the present students are out of school, it's completely conceivable that this country will need a very different kind of prime minister than I am.

"And perhaps that will be sooner than even I think. Or much longer perhaps than many of you wish. Each decade puts forward leaders with different approaches to problems. But a general recipe for a prime ministerial aspirant is to put the respect of people above the respect for institutions . . . "

1975: "The role of a leader in a democratic society is to show the way to the people, but not to be out of touch with them, not to have theoretical ideas which the people are not able to accept at this particular time."

Trudeau speaks about "the need in these changing times where we are to develop new values and even change our institutions. We came into this control situation a couple of months ago and now people are really realizing it's a different world and that you can't live in a different world with the same institutions and the same values that you had before.

"The habits that we've acquired, the behaviours that we've acquired in this two or three hundred years of an industrial society have led to sending the system out of joint.

"Many people ... still see those [wage and price] controls as 'Oh well, it's a bit of strong medicine we'll have to take in order to get inflation down,' but you know it's really more than that ... it's a massive intervention into the decision making process of the economic groups and it's telling Canadians, 'We haven't been able to make it work, the free market system. We've ended up with very high unemployment and very high inflation. We can't go back to what was before with the same habits, the same behaviour and the same institutions.'

"I've seen, well, some economists say, 'All you have to do is get back to the free market system and make this market system work.' It won't you know.

"The way I view it is that we're going to use these three years of controls in order to get people to change and institutions to change."

Trudeau was asked if he thought governments, which were spending 40 per cent of the gross national product, had gone as far as they could.

"Not necessarily, I think at this time, I repeat, we must take a breathing spell. But you have to ask yourselves, the governments are consuming 40 per cent of the GNP, but they're doing it in order to hand out goods and services to the people."

1976: "The truth is that we are living in a new economic era.

"I had thought that the Great Depression of the 1930s had destroyed forever the notion that a free market economy, if unassisted by governments, would produce by itself the ideal state of steady economic growth, stable prices and full employment.

"Every reasonable person now recognizes the duty of the federal government to manage the country's economy in the interests of all its people and all its regions.

"We have a mixed economy which, in the way it has evolved, has served us very well in the past . . . However it is not serving us adequately right now, as the gravity of our problems clearly demonstrates.

"There is a need for structural and rather basic changes in the way we seek to ensure an adequate and reliable supply of the energy and food which are needed . . .

"The problem is not the existence of monopolies or quasi-monopolies in certain sectors of our economy. The problem is how to ensure that their power is used in the public interest and is directed toward the achievement of national goals."

"The control period will . . . give us the necessary time to reform our economic institutions, our attitudes and public policies . . . A call for an immediate start on a national reassessment of our values, our economic institutions . . . to adapt our attitudes and habits to the facts of life."

The Trudeau government issued its working paper, "The Way Ahead", which it called a general paper outlining the economic and social directions the government intends to take after [wage and price] controls end.

"This government has no intention of lessening its commitment to its fundamental social goals. It reaffirms its commitment to a society in which all Canadians can develop their potential to the fullest possible degree . . . New means must be sought to achieve our goals and new policies will be required . . . An important dimension of the task to be accomplished is to achieve a shared appreciation of how the economy works and how governments and individuals can best work together to serve individual and collective economic and social goals.

"One advantage of the controls program is that it provides a 'breathing space' to reflect on the economic direction that would be appropriate after controls are removed."

[Nowhere in the 25-page paper is any reference made to private enterprise or the free market system.]

"The government has concluded . . . that what is ultimately

219

required to meet the challenges of the future goes beyond the introduction of new policy measures to a basic and fundamental reassessment of the role of the government itself.

"The role of the government policy should not be to direct and manage the economy in detail . . . At the same time, however, it must be recognized . . . that the market-directed economic growth has not fully served the social goals and aspirations of Canadians. This government . . . does not intend to participate in, or to allow, a dismantling of the socially progressive society Canadians have built in this country . . . It will therefore be necessary to seek and to implement a broad range of supportive public policies that will enable improved operation of the market economy.

"During this decade [the 1980s] a number of changes in the structure of our economy will be both necessary and desirable . . . It is anticipated that the decade . . . will be a period of important structural price changes . . . If social and economic strains are to be minimized, new directions in which labour-management relations can continue to evolve through the post-control period, becoming more cooperative and less adversarial, are necessary – in both the private and public sectors.

"It will be necessary for labour, management and governments to seek measures that can broaden the scope of labour-management relations and the collective bargaining process in both the private and public sectors.

"Large investments will be required over the coming decades . . . satisfying these capital demands may lead to structural adjustments in the economy . . .

"The concept of a new sharing of social and economic responsibility is fundamental to the search for new directions that will assure balanced growth without inflation."

1977: Trudeau spoke about the need for Canadians to show economic self-restraint and self-discipline.

But, he said, "if they don't discipline themselves, we will discipline them".

1978: "What you can see . . . is a coming of age . . . of the Cana-

dian group, a realization of the new realities – perhaps a ...
readiness to accept change.... We've lived for 110 years without basically changing our constitution. Something like 10 years
ago we embarked upon an exercise to change it fundamentally
... to restructure the power relationships in our society so that
we would indeed be born into a new Canada with a new
constitution giving new distribution of powers and a new arrangement of jurisdictions ... I think Canadians are much more
prepared now to look at basic changes in their constitutional
structures ... There are also certain things that can be done
without the approval of the provinces. We can change the
Senate without the approval of the provinces. We can change
the Supreme Court without the approval of the provinces. We
can entrench certain things in our constitution without the approval of the provinces ... Just two years ago ... I talked about
that type of [economic] challenge and I dared to mention the
word new society, I think, and everybody in the country who
was on a corporate board fell off his chair. Now after visiting
the premiers I've been talking in terms of new methods of
economic policy setting and new economic directions and people are now beginning to see that this is necessary.... Our
economic crisis is forcing us into making the kind of choices
which I think will be great for the future of the country."

1969: Question: "Are you satisfied with some of the shifts we have
made in Canada in the past year?"

Trudeau: "I am satisfied, but I suppose one has to be in the
wheelhouse to see what shifts are taking place. I know that we
have spun the wheel and I know that the rudder is beginning to
press against the waves and the sea ... but perhaps the observer,
who is on the deck and smoking his pipe, or drinking his tea,
sees the horizon much in the same direction and doesn't realize
it, but perhaps he will find himself disembarking at a different
island than the one he thought he was sailing for."

Index

224